Also by Bob Greene:

BE TRUE TO YOUR SCHOOL*

CHEESEBURGERS: The Best of Bob Greene*

GOOD MORNING, MERRY SUNSHINE

AMERICAN BEAT

BAGTIME (with Paul Galloway)

JOHNNY DEADLINE, REPORTER

BILLION DOLLAR BABY

RUNNING: A Nixon-McGovern Campaign Journal

WE DIDN'T HAVE NONE OF THEM FAT FUNKY AN-
GELS ON THE WALL OF HEARTBREAK HOTEL, AND
OTHER REPORTS FROM AMERICA

*Published by Ballantine Books

HOMECOMING

*When the Soldiers
Returned from Vietnam*

Bob Greene

BALLANTINE BOOKS • NEW YORK

Library of Congress Catalog Card Number: 88-26398

ISBN 0-345-36408-2

This edition published by arrangement with G. P. Putnam's Sons

Manufactured in the United States of America

First Ballantine Books Edition: March 1990

*This book is dedicated
to the 2,393 Americans who are still
officially listed as prisoners of war
or missing in action in Vietnam—
with the fervent wish that,
at least for some of them,
there may one day at last
be a homecoming.*

Preface

First, a word about how this book came about.

For years I had been hearing stories that when American troops returned home from Vietnam, they were spat upon by anti-war protesters. The stories were usually very specific. A soldier, fresh from Vietnam duty, wearing his uniform, gets off the plane at an American airport, where he is spat upon by "hippies." For some reason, in the stories it is always an airport where the spitting allegedly happened, and it is always "hippies" who allegedly did the spitting.

In recent years, as we all know, there has been an undeniable shift in the public's attitude toward the men who fought the Vietnam War. The symbols of this new attitude are many—the Vietnam Memorial in Washington is the most dramatic, but the box-office successes of such movies as Platoon *and* Full Metal Jacket *also are testimony that, while the nation may still be divided over the politics of the war, the soldiers themselves are finally being welcomed home with warmth and gratitude.*

Yet even while the country has begun to tell the Vietnam veterans that they are loved and respected, the stories have continued to circulate: when those veterans returned from

Vietnam, they were spat upon. Usually in airports. By hippies.

I began to wonder about that. After all, we knew that the veterans had initially not been greeted with parades and testimonial dinners. So it figured that maybe they had been spat upon.

But did that make sense? Even during the most fervent days of anti-war protest, it seemed that it was not the soldiers whom protesters were maligning. It was the leaders of government, and the top generals—at least that is how it seemed in memory. One of the most popular chants during the anti-war marches was, "Stop the war in Vietnam, bring the boys home." You heard that at every peace rally in America. "Bring the boys home." That was the message.

Also, when one thought realistically about the image of what was supposed to have happened, it seemed questionable. So-called "hippies," no matter what else one may have felt about them, were not the most macho people in the world. Picture a burly member of the Green Berets, in full uniform, walking through an airport. Now think of a "hippie" crossing his path. Would the hippie have the nerve to spit on the soldier? And if the hippie did, would the soldier—fresh from facing enemy troops in the jungles of Vietnam—just stand there and take it?

I raised the question in my syndicated newspaper column. Approximately 2.6 million Americans served in Vietnam. To our lasting sorrow, some 56,000 of them died.

But more than 2 million Vietnam veterans came back alive. It is to those veterans that I posed the question: Were you spat upon when you returned from Vietnam?

I did not ask the question lightly, or out of idle curiosity. It seemed to me that if the spitting-on-soldiers stories were true, we should know it. If they were myth, we should know that, too. I asked the potential respondents to the survey to provide approximate dates, places, and circumstances.

The response was astonishing. From every section and corner of the country, well over a thousand people took the time to sit down, put their thoughts on paper, and tell me what happened when they returned to the U.S. from Vietnam. Virtually no one sent a letter with a simple confirmation or denial of being spat upon; the letters were long, sometimes rambling, invariably gripping essays on what it felt like to come back home after that war.

It was as if by asking that specific, quirky question—"Were you spat upon when you returned?"—I touched a button that would not have been touched had I asked a general question about the homecoming experience. To sum it up quickly, before we get into the letters themselves, I now have no doubt that many returning veterans truly were spat upon—literally—as a part of their welcome home. There were simply too many letters, going into too fine a detail, to deny the fact. I was profoundly moved by how, all these years later, so many men remembered exactly where and when they were spat upon, and how the pain has stayed with them.

On the other hand, many veterans reported stories of kindness and compassion upon their return from Vietnam. Most of this group of veterans said that they believe some of their fellow soldiers were spat upon—but said that they wanted the country to know that, in the late Sixties and the first half of the Seventies, there were American civilians eager to show warmth to returning veterans, too.

Other veterans said they were not spat upon, and were skeptical about the spitting stories. Many more, though, said that the question—if taken literally—was irrelevant. They said that it didn't matter whether a civilian actually worked up sputum and propelled it toward them—they said that they were made to feel small and unwanted in so many other ways that it felt like being spat upon.

As I read the letters, day after day, I came to realize that what I had here was, indeed, much more than a series of *answers to that specific spitting question. The letters made up a sort of oral history of the homecoming experience—a history, in the veterans' own words, of what it was like to return to the U.S. after the most controversial war in the nation's history. Many of the veterans prefaced their letters by saying that they had never before revealed their feelings on the subject. Their emotions ran so deep, they had never wanted to tell anyone.*

My original intention had been to run brief, pithy excerpts from the veterans' responses in my newspaper column—maybe fifteen or twenty little items in a single column, and that would be it. But it became immediately apparent that to do that would be to dishonor the feelings and efforts that the veterans put into telling their stories. As it was, I did a four-part series on the responses, and only managed to excerpt eleven of the more than 1,000 responses. Because of space constraints, even the eleven stories I used had to be drastically boiled down and edited.

When those columns began to run, my phone did not stop ringing. Veterans and civilians, men and women, called in tears to talk about what they were reading. People told me that they had taken the excerpts to private places and had read them in solitude, so that others could not watch them as they reacted to the veterans' words. Several men and women told me that after reading the first set of excerpts, they made a point of getting into their cars, driving to isolated areas, and reading the subsequent excerpts alone so that they would be assured of privacy.

I tried to figure out exactly why the visceral response from readers was so strong. One reason seemed to be the setting— all of the letters had to do with things that had taken place on American soil. Up until now, almost all of the history of the Vietnam soldiers has been placed in the geographical context of Southeast Asia. Somehow, the fact that these sto-

ries happened in the U.S. made them even more compelling to readers.

And, of course, there was the shocking premise behind all of this—the idea that American civilians actually did spit upon returning American soldiers. Undoubtedly this was an unprecedented event in U.S. history, and the fact that it sometimes happened tells us much about the times—perhaps tells us much that we would prefer to forget. To me, though, the value of the letters lay not only in the jarring truths that they told—the value lay in the raging, weeping, prideful, and ultimately triumphant humanity that comes through in the stories.

I knew that these stories must be preserved in permanent form. In telling you about the genesis of the book you now hold in your hands, I have decided to go into several details that you would not normally find in a preface.

When I first spoke with colleagues and friends about the book, one suggestion they offered was that I should go around the country and talk with twelve or fifteen of the letter-writers—that I should make it the story of my journey. A "Bob Greene book," to use a phrase I heard more than once.

I knew what they meant. In the last several years I have written two best-selling books that were based on my own experiences, and in the publishing business—as in other businesses—a time-honored rule is to stick with a successful formula.

But I didn't see the book that way. I wanted readers to be moved the same way I was moved—to read those letters, and to feel the cumulative impact of the soldiers' words. In my mind, I had a picture of the typical veteran who responded to my question. In my mind, he sat in his kitchen, after midnight, and poured his thoughts and memories onto paper. He was not a professional writer; still, he wanted to say it his own way. We are supposedly entering a postliterate age. Yet these veterans all sat down and pulled the stories out of their *souls and their guts. I thought that for me to fly into a handful of towns and to try to make some of the veterans say these things out loud would be a disservice to them. Instead, I wanted to edit their letters—to edit them as gently as I could— so that their voices would come through to the readers of this book with the same impact those voices came through to me.*

That is what I have done. In a number of places throughout the book I have stepped in to offer a few words about my thoughts on the letters—thoughts that you, too, may be having. But the story of Homecoming *is the story told by the letters themselves.*

Another thing you should know—I did not serve in Vietnam. I was of draft age during the era of the Selective Service lottery. My luck was to draw a birthdate number that was never called. How you react to this is up to you—my feelings about it are quite complex, but as I have noted, this is not a book about me. I thought about leaving this information out, but you would have wondered, and you have a right to the answer. I think, for now, I'll leave it at that.

And one more area that is worth explaining. How do we know these letters are "real"? Anyone can pick up a pen or sit down at a typewriter and compose a letter. How do we know that these people even served in the military?

It was a question to which I gave considerable thought. In most of my reporting, I am there to see what is going on. Here, that was not the case. I approached the problem in three ways.

First, any letters that seemed suspect to me—letters which raised a "red flag" in my mind—I did not include in the book. I attempted to err on the side of caution.

Second, I wrote back to every person who had sent me the letters I decided to use here. I told them that I realized they had originally responded to a newspaper column, and that I therefore assumed they had expected their words might show up in the paper. I explained to them that I thought the subject deserved to be treated at book length, and I asked for their permission to use the letters. My feeling was that—on the odd chance that someone had said things in a letter that he knew not to be true—he would not want the letter in the book. The letters you are about to read were all confirmed by the people who wrote them.

Third, I made a number of calls to the Pentagon. I was told that the military's policy is not to give out any information about men and women who have served. It is ironic; the names of the soldiers who gave their lives are there for everyone to see on The Wall in Washington, but the Pentagon is uneasy about even confirming the existence of the men and women who came back alive. I was told that to do so would violate privacy regulations; off the record, I was told that many insurance companies try to obtain the names of Vietnam veterans, and that this is one of the reasons for the policy.

I did, however, find a source in the Veterans Administration who was willing to check out a limited number of names for me. So I went through the letters, and I selected the ones that—even after their writers had corresponded with me for a second time—seemed the slightest bit off. My source confirmed whether these veterans had, indeed, served. I hope that going through all of this does not seem disrespectful to the people who wrote. I just wanted to do everything I could to assure the legitimacy of the letters.

Having said that, is there a chance that a ringer or two will pop up here? Of course. I suppose that is a strange thing to say at the outset of a nonfiction book—but we are dealing with human beings here, and memories, and emotional trauma. I think you will agree, after reading the letters, that even if several should prove to be not what they appear to be, that does not detract from the overall story that is being told.

One final word: Obviously the subject of this book will be of interest to people who served in Vietnam. But if that is all the book is, then it is a waste. This is an American story—a story of an amazing, troubling time in our history that may never be repeated again. In many ways, it is far more important for people who were never in Vietnam to read it than it is for the veterans to read it. The veterans already know the story.

Two young women—Julie Herbick and Susan Falcone— assisted me in the preparation of this book. Both grew up in the years following the Vietnam War. Susan Falcone left me a note one evening. She said that she was moved by "the raw honesty of emotion from individuals I might have stereotyped as unemotional macho men." She said she was impressed and touched by "the non-bravado of many who suffered immeasurable wounds both physical and mental, and who have since put things into amazing perspective and gone on with their lives. I salute them."

And she said this:

"As I filed the letters every day, I began to treat them as very special things—as parts of the lives of very fine individuals. If you've ever seen a military funeral where the flag is folded and given to the family of the veteran, you will understand the reverence I have for the letters. As I touched each letter, I felt as if I was being allowed to touch the life of the person who wrote it."

Now . . . the letters.

☆☆☆☆☆☆☆☆☆☆☆☆☆☆☆☆

"Yes, It Did Happen . . .
It Happened to Me"

There is a certain tone to many of the voices of the veterans whose stories appear in this section. The tone is one of bitterness, anger, and continuing shock. The fact that many of the veterans tell their tales in simple narrative style—simply report what happened to them, as they remember it—makes their accounts all the more jarring.

These are the veterans who say that they were, indeed, spat upon. Think about it: Regardless of what they thought of the war—and as you will see, their opinions varied—the fact is, they went to Vietnam because their country asked them to. They risked their lives and had friends die.

And then . . . to survive their tours of duty, and to step back into America—and to be spat upon? By the people they had assumed they were serving while they were in Southeast Asia?

As full of fury—both implied and stated—as some of these letters are, it is surprising that they are not even more so.

SCOTT BROOKS-MILLER, SPOKANE, WASHINGTON

For several weeks I have wondered about whether to respond to your question. It is now a rainy Sunday morning in Spokane, and obviously I am responding.

Yes, I was spat on. I returned from Vietnam in July of 1970 after a year in country with the 12th and 11th Marines. We flew into Norton Air Force Base in Southern California and, after processing, several of us took a cab to LAX. After saying our farewells, I went to the terminal in which I would catch my flight back to Illinois (I'm from Peoria).

While walking down the corridor, I encountered a young man, no older than myself I'm sure, who looked me in the eye and without hesitation spit on my ribbons. I didn't know what to do. I still don't. For all these years I've remembered that experience.

Yes, I'm bitter, and probably always will be. We were not politicians—most of us couldn't even vote. We simply did what we were asked to do, just as our fathers and grandfathers and all the generations preceding did. But because it was an unpopular war, we took the brunt of the anger of the American people. I was spit on and that moment in time came to symbolize to me the way that the American people felt about me. As far as I'm concerned, let the politicians fight the next war. They aren't getting my sons.

CHESTER J. LEBLANC, LAKE CHARLES, LOUISIANA

From January of 1969 until February of 1970, I was stationed in the city of DaNang, as part of the U.S. Navy's support unit there. In February I returned to the States, where I was separated from active duty at Long Beach, California. After processing, we were driving to the Los Angeles International Airport.

While walking down one of the concourses, I was stopped

by a young lady wearing typical flower child attire—a long maxi-dress, with granny-type glasses. She stopped me and, seeing my campaign ribbons, asked if I had been in Vietnam. When I told her I was just coming from there, she spat upon my uniform and ran off.

I had a military duffel bag slung over one shoulder, and I was carrying a briefcase in the other hand. I immediately dropped both articles and proceeded to run after her. After running about twenty yards, I stopped, said a couple of choice curse words, and thought: Welcome home.

DAVID S. WEICK, BLOOMFIELD, NEW MEXICO

The five of us met in Oakland after we flew back from Vietnam, and were waiting to process out of the Army next morning. We got in around 11 p.m. on the 14th of June, 1969. The next day, while we were wandering around getting the necessary outprocessing physicals and pay, we all decided to go over to Fisherman's Wharf and have a "We made it home alive" dinner together, and then we would go our separate ways and that would be that.

We all had steak and lobster and split a bottle of wine. After the dinner we were standing outside on the sidewalk, saying good-bye, when somewhere up the street somebody lit and threw a bunch of firecrackers, which caused all five of us to hit the deck and start low-crawling for some sort of cover. I think we all realized where we were at the same time and proceeded to stand up and look at each other, feeling more than a little foolish.

About this time a guy in his mid-twenties walked up. He looked at each of us in turn, said, "You fucking baby killers don't look so bad," and then he spit on me, I guess since I was the closest to him. Before he could spit on anyone else, or for that matter do anything, he was hit, spun around, and we all took a poke at him. The thought hit us that while we were "out of the Army," we were still governed for the next seventy-two hours by military regulations, and could in all probability get court-martialed or receive some sort of punishment from the Army, so we beat feet.

As we walked away, the people who had seen what happened gave us a round of applause, and that was that. We all went our way to catch planes home. Today I couldn't tell you any of their names.

DAVID McTAMANEY, NEWBURGH, NEW YORK

After a year of unbelievable hell in Vietnam, I was at the "repo depo" in Long Binh awaiting my flight out. The last thing I was told by the sergeant in charge as we boarded the aircraft was not to expect any welcome home committees when we got off the plane.

I arrived at Oakland Air Force Base on April 14 (my mother's birthday), 1970. I had sat near the front of the plane, and therefore was one of the first to get off. As I looked out toward the terminal, I noticed a large crowd, maybe 200 or so people, on the far side of a cyclone wire fence. In front of them, on our side of the fence, were MPs, wearing ponchos. As we started to file out of the plane, the MPs shouted to us to move quickly, and began holding up their ponchos.

We were in khaki short-sleeved uniforms, and I was surprised that it would be raining in California. As I got closer to the MPs and the crowd, I still could not make out what they were yelling. Then the first egg landed near my foot. At first, like a fool, I looked up in the air, still not putting together what was going on. As my ears popped, adjusting to the change in pressure, I began to hear for the first time the chant: "How many babies did you kill today?"

Several of them were leaning against the fence, spitting at us and at the MPs blocking their view. Others were heaving eggs over the fence and into our midst. The MPs were covered with spittle and eggs, which explained the ponchos. They were obviously used to this ritual. The fellow behind me said, "Jesus, I wish I had brought my M-16!," and my stomach dropped as I realized for the first time what was going on.

I stopped to ask one of the MPs who these people were, and as I did so a woman about forty years old, not a teenager by any stretch of the imagination, leaned back and spit on me with all her strength. It landed on my shirt pocket, near the ribbons that I was wearing for the first time. "Bull's-eye!" she yelled. An MP lieutenant took my arm and said, "Go inside, son, and ignore them."

I was reunited with my duffel bag, shoved my records under my arm, and headed for home. To get to Albany, New York, where my wife was attending graduate school and working in the college library, required a two-hour stopover in O'Hare Airport in Chicago.

Walking through O'Hare made me more uncomfortable than walking through the paddies and jungles. People, all ages, pointed and laughed, made snide and derogatory comments, and turned to watch me go by. I could understand if I had been sloppy drunk, but I was cold sober and could have passed inspection. I had traveled in airports when I was in college, and I never recall people acting like this. Of course, I hadn't been in uniform at that time.

I sat down in a remote corner to wait, and a young woman looked up, grabbed her small child and her suitcase, said, "You ought to be ashamed of yourself!" and moved to another seating area. I actually looked to see if my fly was open or if I was inadvertently doing something that may have offended her. I sat there for about half an hour and noticed that the opposite end of the seating area was quite crowded, but no one was sitting in any of the chairs near me. I offered my seat to one older lady, who looked me up and down and said, quite deprecatingly, "I'd rather stand."

I grabbed my stuff and headed for the bathroom. My first thought was to get out of my uniform, and I remember trying to figure out if I had brought home anything with me that I could wear in early April in Chicago (I was already freezing in my khakis). Military regulations required that one wear his uniform when flying on military standby, but I knew I had enough money to pay the difference in the fare and get to Albany as quickly as possible.

As I entered the bathroom, a young guy, about twenty or so, wearing a headband and a leather vest, stepped back and looked at me.

"Have you been in Vietnam?" he asked innocently.

"Yeah," I said, "I just got back, and I'm heading home to Al—"

He never let me finish. He leaned back, made a couple of swishing motions with his mouth, and spit in my face. I jumped backward, but his spittle hit me on my bare arm.

I took a step forward, realizing that he couldn't escape, and felt my heart begin to pump faster. I felt myself getting ready to rip him to pieces. Instead—and I still don't know why—I let him walk past me. I went to the sink and washed off my arm. I dragged all my stuff into the toilet stall, locked the door, put my face in my hands, and cried for the first time in months.

RONALD L. TROUSDALE, LAS VEGAS, NEVADA

I take no pleasure in a "Yes, I was spat upon" vote, but here it is.

In June or July of 1969 I was going to take a college entrance exam at Palomar College near Oceanside, California. I had plans of going on to college in the fall after getting an early out from the Marines. While waiting on the steps leading from the parking lot, I was approached by a female and two males—average looking, nicely dressed, 17 or 18 years old.

The girl asked if I was in the Marines—I guess because of my haircut. I said yes. She then said, "Have you been to Vietnam?" I again said yes. She said, "So you're one of those baby killers." Then one of the boys spit on me, hitting my neck and shirt collar.

I punched at him while his buddy ran away and his girl-friend screamed at me, calling me all kinds of vulgarities.

I didn't take those exams. I just drove back to Camp Pen-dleton, as I had no desire to be further reviled by my fellow countrymen, for what I perceived to be a hatred of those of us who served this country.

I still feel the slime on my neck.

FREDERICK H. GIESE, ARLINGTON HEIGHTS, ILLINOIS

I was medically evacuated from Vietnam in November, 1969, to a Naval hospital in Japan where, after my recovery, I was stationed. During my tour there I married a Japanese lady and adopted her son. She became pregnant; in early 1970 I was transferred back to the U.S.A.

My family and I landed at San Francisco International Airport after a very long flight from Japan. We were going into the cafeteria to eat and, of course, I was in my uniform with all my Vietnam medals, including the Purple Heart and the Gold Star.

My family and I were standing in line, when, out of the blue, this middle-aged lady walked up to me with a bowl of potato salad in her hand. She threw the salad smack in the middle of my chest and spat what salad she had in her mouth in my face. Then she proceeded to call me a "baby killer," "war monger" and a lot of other vile names.

I became so angry and humiliated that I balled my hands into fists and would have hit this "lady," had it not been for two other servicemen who grabbed me and got me out of there. I'm glad they did get me out of there before I'd had the time to react, because I later thought about headlines that could have read: "Crazed Vietnam Vet Assaults Middle-Aged Woman."

That is how I was welcomed home. That is how my family was first introduced to America.

This "lady" was no hippie. I sort of get the feeling it has been easy to "blame" hippies for things like this because they were easily identifiable, and because they did dramatically, in many cases, communicate their opposition to the Vietnam war. But the verbal and physical abuse of returning Vietnam veterans took place in all levels of American society.

PAUL EDWARD JENKINS, CINCINNATI, OHIO

In early February of 1972, I was in the Honolulu airport—in uniform—with 200-plus other GIs who were returning to the world. We were in Hawaii for a refueling; it was our first step on American soil, and it was very late at night.

Told to report back to the plane in an hour, the vast majority of us headed immediately for a cold one in the airport lounge. Stopping to buy a newspaper, I ended up about fifty feet behind the line moving toward the bar.

Two young guys—complete with beards, long hair, John Lennon glasses and garbed in the appropriate apparel that the times dictated—came into sight. It occurred to me that one of them resembled my best friend back home.

One fellow was leaning against the wall, the other half-kneeling, half-sitting on the floor. Their backpacks were beside them, and it was rather obvious that they were simply waiting on a plane. They weren't really protesting much of anything. No signs. Nothing.

My initial thought was, wow, "real people." And although I was a bit conservative at the time, I thought, "my people." It was great to be home.

As I drew nearer, they began with some remarks and grins to each other, and then directed them toward me. Their remarks and tone escalated very quickly from crude, to rude, to vulgar.

"My people" were angry. At me. It blew me away.

It would be ludicrous, all these years later, to pretend to remember exactly what was said. But there is no forgetting the spitting.

They aimed at my feet. They missed. I kept walking, to the tune of "baby killer, baby killer."

Stand there and take it? Yes. I took it. It never occurred to me to do anything else.

When I entered the bar, I found several waitresses wiping ashtrays, and a bartender explaining to 200 Vietnam veterans that the lounge had closed five minutes earlier, and she was really sorry, but no, they couldn't serve us coffee, either.

MARION WELLER, SAN ANTONIO, TEXAS

Some of us had been up for almost 48 hours, going from Vietnam and then from airport to airport. Several of us flew from Seattle to Chicago. At the Chicago airport, several unkempt and unrestrained hippies, in their twenties, I think, boarded our plane. They handled the medals on several of the men's uniforms, they spit on us, and called us really obscene names. On the plane, one of these creeps kept goading a Marine corporal, and actually held a lighted cigarette to his uniform. It was to the Marine's credit that he didn't kill the guy then and there—I really wanted to. We were heckled when we got to the Philadelphia airport, too.

We were all really too tired to maybe notice closely the significance. It hit us later.

DR. ROBERT A. FINK, BERKELEY, CALIFORNIA

It happened to me, and it was no joke.

In September of 1967, I was called to active duty with the U.S. Army Medical Corps. I was a neurosurgeon then (as I am now), and had recently completed a postdoctoral fellowship at the University of California at Berkeley. I was fortunate during my military service (two years of active duty) to be stationed at a large hospital facility stateside—although I did not actually go to Vietnam, I was responsible for the treatment of a large number of wounded Vietnam soldiers.

I was stationed at Letterman General Hospital in San Francisco, and I commuted between the hospital and my home in Berkeley. This was during the time when demonstrations and anti-war sentiment were at their peak. I, too, opposed the Vietnam war, and this made for some very interesting interchanges during my time in the Army; but I must say that a certain amount of disagreement was accepted by the military, and I had very little negative feedback from my Army colleagues during my two years. The probable reason behind this was the fact that we were all physicians, and looked upon our service as a healing one; and besides, most of us felt that it was, indeed, our obligation to help our country even though we did not always agree with what our country was doing.

In any case, when I would come home from the hospital (of course wearing my uniform, which was required), I would receive many negative comments from other residents of Berkeley. One afternoon a youngster, approximately twelve years old, who lived across the street from us, literally spat on me as I got out of my car. He shouted, "How many did you kill today?"

You can imagine how I felt—especially since I had spent that day trying to reconstruct the skull of a Vietnam soldier who had suffered severe shrapnel wounds, and who had recently been transferred back to the United States for surgery.

At a later date, I sat down with the young man who had spat on me and clarified some things with him. I think that resolved the issue, but I will never forget that incident.

There was, indeed, another incident of that type, even though it did not involve spitting. One day on the way to the hospital from home in the early morning rush hour, I developed a case of gastrointestinal upset. After being caught in traffic for a while, I found myself in an urgent situation where I needed to use a public restroom. I pulled into a service station near the hospital, and went to use the facilities—but was told that unless I purchased gasoline, the facilities were closed. I was wearing the uniform of the United States, and they refused to allow me to use the restroom.

LAURENCE W. HOWENSTEIN, NORTH AURORA, ILLINOIS

I returned home from Vietnam in August of 1968, after serving with the Green Berets. Barely 60 hours after leaving the jungle, I was "home"—Chicago's O'Hare Airport.

The aircraft arrived ahead of schedule and we sat somewhere off the runway while other aircraft offloaded. By the time I departed the plane, we were one hour late. The people who were to meet me were not there; I learned when I called home that they had left the airport, believing they had missed me.

I was not overjoyed to be greeted by the people who were there to "meet" me. There was a group of about six people who were speaking against our involvement in Vietnam. It was not a quiet group discussion, but a loud voicing of their opinion.

Most of my fellow passengers were met by someone and hurried off to claim their baggage, while I was standing there trying to locate my family. The male members of the group approached me. I ignored them and whatever they were saying. I started to walk by them, and they threw toward me a wadded-up paper. One of them had a mouth full of liquid that he spat toward me. I remember they called me a baby killer and a murderer.

I remember I was mad at them for what they just said and did to me. I would probably have broken their bodies, but as I started toward them one of the women came to me and handed me something, I do not remember what, and said something to the order of let there be peace in the world.

I turned away and called home. While I was waiting for my family to pick me up, she came over to me. I told her I had nothing to say to her or her friends, and to keep them away from me.

ALVIN L. LONG, WIMBERLEY, TEXAS

For the record, I was a two-tour Vietnam vet, 1969–1970 and 1972–1973. In April of 1970, when I was returning home from Vietnam, a "lady" spat at me in the airport in San Francisco. She also called me a baby killer, which was probably true.

Do not kid yourself, the peace movement was not just against the government, but also against us fools who served this country loyally.

The American people can go to hell before I or my sons fight another war for them.

TONY J., SAN FRANCISCO, CALIFORNIA

When I got back to the U.S. I had what they called burial detail. That's when you had to escort a person's body back to his next of kin and represent the U.S. and tell them their son, husband or whoever had given his life for his country and you had to stick around until he was buried—you were there to make sure the next of kin was okay.

Well, I had to take this fellow's body to his wife—she was

nineteen years old. It was in 1966 and his home was in Sacramento. I'm withholding his name and mine, just out of respect to his family. If they read this it would only open up a lot of old wounds, and they have suffered enough. That's the only reason for that.

But to get to the bad part, I was helping the mortician take the casket out of the hearse. Of course I was in my dress uniform, medals and all that, and the American flag was over the casket and some guy walked by when we had it out about halfway and the fool spit on it and said, "Good, he deserved to die."

I couldn't drop the casket, but as soon as we had it out of the hearse I told the mortician to put it down and I just took off running after the fool. But he was long gone by that point. Now I think back on it and am glad I didn't catch him. I'd probably still be in jail for murder.

Here was a true young American who had given his life just for someone to come up and spit on him. No way! It just hurt and upset me—I'll never forget it. As for those war movies about Vietnam, they really hurt when they are pretty close to what happened over there. But of course Hollywood has made it seem like it was neat being there. Bull!!

KENNETH M. BALL, LITTLETON, COLORADO

Yes, Vietnam veterans were spat upon. At least one was. Date: Spring 1970. Place: Albuquerque, New Mexico; University of New Mexico campus; Mechanical Engineering Building. Occasion: Campus-wide demonstration following the Kent State shootings. Recipient of spit: The writer, age 24 at the time, senior in mechanical engineering, attempting to get to class for a scheduled exam, and having returned ten months previously from the ammo dumps of Vietnam. Spitter: Female, age perhaps nineteen or twenty, braless, overweight, unwashed. Part of an "activist" group which sat three-deep against the college doors. Results: Took the exam, then went back to my part-time job. Entire university of 20,000 was closed and spring semester was abbreviated. I believe the words used were, "Goddamned fascist baby-killer."

CLAUDE A. SMITH, GAITHERSBURG, MARYLAND

During August of 1966, while I was assigned for duty in the Munitions Building on Constitution Avenue in Washington, D.C., I was spat upon by a complete stranger while returning from lunch.

I was in a Class A uniform, a CWO in the Army, walking along the street when I passed this man in casual civilian dress. As he passed he spat and made a remark: "You dirty (obscenity) killer."

I didn't realize he had spit on me at first, and decided not to cause a scene over what he had said. But I noticed his spit on my tie shortly after. His only possible provocation was my being a soldier in the uniform of my country.

He was not a hippie. He could have been a tourist, and both he and I were alone walking in opposite directions. I had never seen the man before.

As a result of this instance and to avoid other problems, our commanding officer encouraged us to wear civilian attire to work instead of our uniforms.

JIM PEPPER, AUSTIN, TEXAS

Yes, it did happen. It happened to me—and on more than one occasion.

I served in Southeast Asia in 1971–72, and was shipped home and arrived at Los Angeles International Airport on December 23, 1972. I had to remain in the Los Angeles area, in uniform, for two days just prior to Christmas Day awaiting paper work and my discharge from the U.S. Marine Corps.

The day I arrived, in the first bar I went into while still at the airport, I was confronted by a group of loud and obnoxious "longhairs" who took offense to my having entered the bar, in uniform. They name-called, jeered, and generally confronted me with taunting insults until I chose to leave and go elsewhere. They followed my withdrawal from the bar, en masse, and spit on the floor in contempt of me and my uniform, and verbalized all sorts of diverse negative opinions of me and what they thought I represented. I walked away.

A short time later, while at home after my discharge, I wore my jungle utilities uniform on a "walk-a-thon," where we all hiked down the highway attempting to walk several miles to raise money to save Bald Eagle nesting areas. While on that walk-a-thon, two motorcycle riders actually turned around and rode back to me. They took exception to my wearing of that "combat" uniform. They digressed into name-calling and other verbal abuse and then spit "at" me— although the spittle did not actually hit me. They "fled" on their motorcycles; I continued my walk.

An additional point: I, as I am sure was the case with most others in uniform at the time, was ordered to avoid confrontations with civilians, and frankly didn't give a damn about their opinions at that moment in my life.

HARLAN L. BAKKE, DENVER, COLORADO

I returned from Vietnam in September of 1965, arriving at Travis Air Force Base about 3 a.m. I asked about the transit quarters, but was told they were full—but there was an empty building with mattresses on the floor we could use until morning.

Four of us grabbed a cab and went downtown to see lights, cars, round eyes, etc. The first stop was a convenience store to get a quart of milk (fresh, not reconstituted). The first results, I got sick because I was not used to fresh milk. We got a hotel room, and didn't get to the Oakland Army Terminal until the next day.

Friday evening about 7:30 p.m. I received my separation papers and started out for San Francisco Airport. Because it was late and there were no cabs around, I carried my duffel bag to the freeway. Because it was required to get discharged in uniform, there I was standing on the freeway in uniform, carrying my duffel bag.

After some time, a car stopped about fifty feet ahead of me. I grabbed my bag and ran up to the car. I leaned over to look in the window and asked if they were going near the airport. There were four guys in the car (not overly long hair). I heard one say something about "Army pigs" and something else. As the car started moving, the guy in the back seat rider side spat on me, and the car drove off. After some time an empty cab came by and I went to the airport. The next day I got a flight home to Minneapolis.

I and others adopted a travel procedure as follows:

(1) Never travel in uniform.
(2) Never tell anyone you are in the service.
(3) Never wear G.I. shoes, or they will know.

DAVID H. MORRISON, FORT BRAGG, CALIFORNIA

While back in my hometown of Everett, Massachusetts, three months back from Nam, I was hitchhiking to get to the Boston Naval Shipyard. I don't remember the date— sometime in spring 1968. I was in uniform and a car slowed as if to pick me up. The passenger rolled down his window, spit on me, flipped me off, and yelled something. The people in the car were my age and I don't know if they were hippies.

There is something people do not understand about coming home from the bush. People have the picture of a burly

Green Beret. We were not all Green Berets. I went to Nam weighing 240 and came back 180. I had seen enough violence and was in shock from the seventy-two hours of travel.

My image of home was the same as it was when I had left. That is one of the things that kept me going—life would be better when I returned home, and there would be no need to be violent anymore. But just as I had changed, this country had changed. We all have to answer the questions from that war.

TED PODOLAK, MENTOR, OHIO

I returned to "the world" in September 1969. It was a different world than the one I came from.

After 14 months in Vietnam, it took 48 hours for me to leave the country, process out of the Army in California, and be sitting in the Chicago airport.

I was wearing my uniform, campaign medals, with stitches above my eye and my arm in a sling from war injuries.

A group of three or four young college types, about 17 to 21 years old (not "hippie" but activist), made some derogatory remarks toward me. One of them spat in my direction, missing me, but making their meaning very clear.

Their gesture confused and hurt me. I would have cried if my emotions had not been so numb.

Little did I suspect that my emotions would remain confused to this day.

GEORGE M. HOUSEHOLDER, PAINESVILLE, OHIO

A man in the service, especially one who has been outside the United States during the time when the hair and lifestyles changed so drastically, has a tendency to refer to all those people who strive to be different as "hippies" and "bums." The need for attention makes them dress and act the way they do whether or not they truly believe in anything. They say and do things that will get them attention. Harassing a serviceman is equivalent to harassing a policeman, or any other Establishment figure.

Okay. Here goes. . . .

In June 1969, the LST I was on sustained implosion damage from the grenades used to ward off "zappers." The damage required dry docking, and the ship was sent to Japan. I had been overseas for 19 months already, and the majority of that time was spent in Vietnam. I got lucky and was able to get a hop all the way from Yokota, Japan, to Wright-Patterson AFB, Ohio, which was great, considering home was a suburb of Cleveland.

I was sitting in a chair in the Columbus airport talking to some of the infantrymen who had hopped in with me, passing time. We had some girls come over to us and one or two hippies had a word or two to say, but we ignored them (not the girls, of course). After you have been overseas as long as some of us had, American girls were something special.

Shortly thereafter another hippie-type person came over to us, stood directly in front of where I was sitting and, in language flowered with the best vernacular of the day, was pointing at our service ribbons and other accoutrements, and calling us sarcastically "war heroes." He then proceeded to spout a line I had not heard before, but I would live to hear over and over: He called us "baby burners." At that point he spat on me. I'm sure he never expected the response he got. As a reflex action, I sprang up and put his lights out. It was the proverbial two-hit fight.

Before I even realized what I had done, one of the local constabulary had grabbed me and was escorting me to the Security Room, despite the objections of the other servicemen present. The person I hit was not detained even a moment. He was helped to his feet, asked if he was okay, and summarily dismissed. They didn't even ask him if he wanted to press charges.

In the Security Room I was told that I would be transferred to Columbus and would have to be arraigned. Charges such as disorderly conduct and assault and battery would be made. My justifications and the circumstances that I was trying to get home were ignored.

A chief petty officer, whose name I never got and I'm not exactly sure whether he was part of the local Shore Patrol or just a concerned serviceman, in his eloquence or blarney, was able to convince the police to allow me to go on my way. I think the only reason they did, in fact, let me go was because they had neglected to have the guy sign a complaint or press charges. But that again is something I will never know for sure.

When my flight was ready to depart I was escorted to the airplane and allowed to continue my trip home.

Looking back on things, it is obvious to me now that the guy who spit on me was performing for the others nearby. At the time, that fact was given no consideration.

I may not be the best storyteller in the world, but I will tell this story as long as I feel people need to hear it.

CHRIS RAMEL, DENVER, COLORADO

I think the date was March 7, 1972. I was in the San Francisco airport. I had just showered and put a fresh uniform (Air Force) on for my first leg home. Walking out to my gate I passed a ''hippie'' who spat upon me and continued walking in the opposite direction, without a word.

I made nothing of the incident for two reasons:

(1) I was happy to be going home after 367 days in Thailand, and didn't want anything to screw it up, and

(2) Officers who get in public fights, while in uniform, are dealt with in a fairly severe fashion.

LOU ROCHAT, UNIVERSAL CITY, TEXAS

In January 1969 I joined the Army due to a draft declassification back to 1A while attending college at Texas Wesleyan in Fort Worth. It seems I completed a one-year technical school after graduating from high school in Mineral Wells, and that was all the college I was going to be allowed to receive. My draft notice came a few days after I joined.

We enlisted swine were transported by bus to Fort Polk, Louisiana for basic training. No contact with the public. After basic, we who had enlisted for helicopter flight training were taken by bus again to Fort Wolters, Texas, for flight training. After five months at Wolters, you were on your own to get to Fort Rucker, Alabama to finish flight school. No one wore their uniforms going there even though the GI haircut was a dead giveaway. Rucker was so far out in the woods that sunlight had to be pumped in. Again, no place to go, so stay on base and out of trouble with the locals, including Panama City, where all the girls were.

Four months of Rucker and you were now an officer in the U.S. Army and a pilot. You went to one of two places after graduation in January 1970: Nam, or additional flight training, then Nam. I went to Savannah, Georgia for helicopter gunship training before going to Nam. The people there tolerated you because you were an "officer" and made good money, which you naturally spent freely. Don't get caught with a local's daughter, though, or you'll be gator food.

April 1970 and I am at the airport in Dallas on my way to Nam. The airport Bible flippers wouldn't even approach you because of the uniform. I think "Mother fuckin' baby killer" was the favorite line we heard. In Frisco, we had to change flights with a one hour wait. I was spit on twice—once by a female hippie-type who smelled as bad as she looked and secondly by a well dressed young business type who would be called a "yuppie" today. Him I flattened with a left hook in the gut and a right to his big mouth. My fellow officers and I were escorted to our plane by security and held there until the plane left. The average American in the airport only called us names without any physical violence threatened. Terms such as "Murderer," "Baby killer," "Mercenary asshole," "Rapist," and "Fucking Bastard War Monger" were the parting words from our fellow Americans we were getting ready to die for.

These taunts came from men and women, young and old. The rest of our trip was uneventful, as our stops in Hawaii and Guam were monitored by security police and we weren't allowed to wander off while the plane was being refueled.

Vietnam was Vietnam. I came back on a stretcher with seven bullet holes in me, 57 combat decorations (two Silver Stars), and spent two years in an Army hospital due to my service.

Some of my friends that didn't come back on military Medevac told me the name-calling and spitting got them again in Frisco and other major airports. We all resolved this in our future assignments by not wearing our uniforms in public. This worked well, because the Army was letting us wear our hair longer and we purchased civilian-type luggage and did not use the bags issued to us by the military. As long as you didn't look like the military, you were left alone.

Something else, our feelings about Kent State and the shootings: They didn't shoot enough of those students!

My feelings now? America better not get in a war outside of Texas because I won't show up for it. The bad guys cross the Texas border and I'll be there, but nowhere else.

Oh, yeah, while in Nam I did kill quite a few of the enemy including grenade-toting kids and AK47-packing women. I don't feel bad about it at all, in fact, it felt great, after digging parts of my fellow aviation people out of the ground or untying their body parts from trees where they were dissected after being shot down and caught alive. I would have stayed in Nam until the end if I hadn't been shot so bad, but it was over by the time I got back to active duty.

If we ever do go to war again and I decide to participate if the Army will have me, I'll shoot every SOB who curses me or spits on me for defending our country.

WILLIAM VODDEN, ST. CHARLES, ILLINOIS

I was a Marine sergeant. This is factual information. It did happen to me. I was coming home through Travis Air Force Base in California, taking a connecting flight to Chicago out of Oakland. We returned early in the morning (September 1972) and were "greeted" by a handful of hippies who were demonstrating outside the base. As we left they did indeed spit. Nice welcome home! This is true information and not made up.

J. LEONARD CALDEIRA, CHICAGO, ILLINOIS

The circumstances of my being spat upon were somewhat different than the stereotype, and, frankly, I never realized that there were other veterans complaining of similar occurrences.

I served in Vietnam during the height of the war, September 1967 to September 1968. If you recall, the war sentiment at the time was such that when I went to Vietnam I was still considered by many to be a patriot. By the time I was ready to return home, the United States had experienced the Chicago Democratic Convention, the riots in Detroit, the assassinations of Martin Luther King Jr. and Bobby Kennedy, the riots in many cities—and Haight Ashbury in San Francisco had blossomed. Frankly, I felt safer in Vietnam.

When I returned from overseas duty, I was to leave the Army and "outprocess" in San Francisco. My girlfriend, who became my fiancée in San Francisco and now has been my wife for eighteen years, met me upon my arrival. One day while simply touring the San Francisco area, in uniform, a rather nondescript man on the street spit at my uniform because he was obviously in disagreement with what it represented at the time. Nothing was said, but the incident saddened and confused me. I took off my uniform later that day and never put it on again during the rest of my stay in San Francisco.

What bothered me the most about the incident was that, having been born in 1944, I grew up with World War II movies which made soldiers heroes, and always showed them coming home to ticker-tape parades down Fifth Avenue. If there is any aspect of the war that I had trouble coping with, it was trying to understand spitting on a uniform. I was an officer involved in covert intelligence work in Vietnam, so I did not experience some of the horrors of the infantrymen who were in the heat of battle every day. The only "mental scar" that remains with me today of Vietnam was the unwelcome display of that man in San Francisco.

I had effectively put the incident out of my mind to the point that I do not remember anything about the man except that he was *not* a hippie. Until now, I always thought my experience was somewhat isolated.

M. TIERNY, LAS VEGAS, NEVADA

I attended a military reunion in New York in 1968. I was standing in front of the Waldorf waiting for a cab when a young girl walked up to me and spat. She said something and walked away.

The doorman told me that it was not a "good idea" to wear a uniform in New York.

ROBERT E. MCCLELLAND, MASSILLON, OHIO

Yes, I am a Vietnam veteran who was spat upon—literally and figuratively. By hippies? I don't know. In the airport? Yes. San Francisco International Airport on October 11, 1971 at 3:15 p.m., and yes, I was still in uniform. To be exact, it was the same uniform that I wore during the last Fire Support Mission I was involved in, just 36 hours before landing in San Francisco Airport. No, I didn't have mud, dirt, or gunpowder on my uniform. A very kind Vietnamese woman at the Transit Company washed and ironed it for me so that I could come home to the country I love looking nice. This was one hell of a lot more than I received upon arrival.

If I were the only one to be spat upon, the score would be: not spat upon, 1,999,999, spat upon, 1. Of course, I know this score to be wrong. Literally because I saw others spat on, and figuratively because to spit on one Vietnam veteran is to spit on them all.

The person who spat on me was wearing a shirt that said "Welcome Home Baby Killer." Now I am sure that this person did not represent all the people in the U.S. In fact, I know this, because my wife and family didn't spit on me and call me a baby killer. Of course, why would they? They know me. They know I was only doing what my country asked me to.

I was young, 20, when I went to Vietnam; I was there for a year and came back 21 going on 50. No joke intended here. I was so confused when the girl in the mall asked me if I just came back from Florida because I had such a nice tan. Then she moved a couple of steps away from me and stopped talking when I said, "No, back from Vietnam."

Did you see "Platoon?" Try living what you saw in "Platoon" for a year. Go from that to McDonald's hamburgers, fast cars, and flush toilets in just 36 hours. Have you ever had a 12-year-old kid ask you, "How many people did you get to kill, mister?'' Try a few scenes like that and see if you feel spat upon.

I am sure by now you think I am probably one of those Vietnam veterans who sit in a bar all day and can't hold down a job. Wrong. I own an auto repair business and employ six other people.

About that image of a burly Green Beret walking through the airport and being spat upon by a war protester—let's also remember that most war protesters or hippies or whatever name you want to attach to them were also becoming very aware of their rights as U.S. citizens, and they knew that if this burly Green Beret did nothing they (protesters) had won, and if the burly Green Beret retaliated, they (protesters) still won. How could they lose?

For fifteen years I put Vietnam behind me by working 12 hours a day and telling myself that it couldn't get to me because I wouldn't let it. Then the tough guy started to fall apart. My wonderful wife of sixteen years couldn't do anything right, and I was about to lose her and my three children. After some of my friends (Vietnam veterans) told me that it wasn't her that had changed, it was me, I went to three doctors to find out what was happening to me. I ended up at the Veterans Clinic talking to a psychiatrist, who told me this was very typical post-traumatic stress and depression from Vietnam. My wife (very understanding and supportive) and I are working on putting things back together while I am trying to learn to deal with my problems. Yes, my problems—not yours, or the U.S. government's, or the hippies', or the war protesters', or the girl at the mall's, or my employees', or my customers', or my children's. For God's sake and by His Grace, never my children's, yours, or anyone's.

ROSE MARIE MCDONOUGH, GREEN BAY, WISCONSIN

I am a female veteran of the U.S. Air Force—1967, 1968, 1969, and 1970. I was in Southeast Asia though not actually in Vietnam. I returned to the States in 1970 through Travis Air Force Base, and from there I visited a friend for a week and then flew back to the Midwest through O'Hare. I worked at a vegetable canning factory and at a local ski resort before returning to college at the University of Wisconsin, Madison, in the fall of 1971. This is where my spitting story takes place.

I had joined a veterans' group called Vets for Peace. We were active in anti-war protest marches in Milwaukee, Madison and Chicago. We usually marched with a group of veterans from Chicago called Vietnam Veterans Against the War. It was in Madison, on Veterans Day, 1971, as I was walking to the Capitol building from campus (all alone). I was wearing my Air Force overcoat and my Vets for Peace hat when a man about 19 or 20 years old looked me in the face and spit right into my face. He was a normal looking man, nothing to distinguish him from a thousand other people. But I will never forget what he did to me.

WALTER HOWARD, ROSELLE, ILLINOIS

Not only was I spat upon. I was also cursed, egged, and booed. Please excuse my terrible penmanship. At the moment I am trying to watch my two-year-old son.

FATHER GUY MORGAN, FORT COLLINS, COLORADO

I am a retired Catholic chaplain who served the Air Force community for twenty years. I had two tours in Vietnam (Phan Rang and Bien Hoa). I left Bien Hoa on November 18,

1968, flew military contract aircraft to Philadelphia, and then on to New York for two weeks' leave.

While I was leaving the JFK airport to catch a bus to the city, a lady (around 43 years old) told me that "I napalm babies" and she spit on me. I didn't take her for a "hippie," though.

Needless to say, she ruined my two weeks' leave.

WILLIAM H. SYDNOR, RICHMOND, VIRGINIA

I'm not a writer to newspaper columnists. I belong to no Vietnam veterans' organizations. It was just last summer that I finally saw the war memorials in D.C. But I have gotten out of bed at 6:30 a.m. to immediately respond to your column despite the fact that it will make me late for work.

The general impression of the Vietnam veteran is remarkably naive and "Hollywoodish." Most of the 2 million veterans of the war were not "burly Green Berets"; nine-tenths of us never fought enemy troops in the jungles. I was assigned to the Long Binh hospital.

My military flight from Vietnam landed at an Air Force base in northern California in the summer of 1971. Within 24 hours I went on leave and was bused to San Francisco International Airport. Since I had an eight hour wait before my flight to Atlanta, I decided to go into town and ride the trolleys—something I had remembered as a joyful experience from an earlier, pre-draft visit to San Francisco.

All soldiers were required to wear their uniforms if they were to receive standby rates on the airlines. I didn't bother to change my clothes to go into town for a few hours. Sitting in the trolley car trying to get back into the mood of America, I was spit on by a group of people who jumped off the car. At first I was simply stunned. Then, perhaps because I was alone and there were four or five of them, I didn't chase after them. But I think more importantly, I was trying to drain all the tension and bad feelings out of myself. Fighting was the last thing on my mind and was my last desire. I was glad to be home. I had left the fighting behind.

If all 2 million veterans were ready to fight at the drop of a hat, or the splat of some spittle, this country would indeed have had a mess on its hands.

From my perspective, the major reason for these spitting stories was that the vast majority of the returning veterans came through California, the most fervent anti-war state, and to get their standby rates they had to be wearing their uniforms. Most of us had within the past 48 hours taken a 20-hour flight across the Pacific. This was the day the majority of us had looked forward to for many months. Do most people fight on the day of their weddings, or the day they graduate from high school or college? Fist fighting in the streets wasn't really high on our list of activities—thus, in my mind, the lack of pugilistic responses.

I grew up with a lot of privilege. Therefore, when I was drafted, I simply felt I had no right to refuse to answer my country's call for help. I have no respect for many of my associates, and even friends, who "cleverly" avoided the draft. They got a head start on life on us draftees, and many got way ahead, particularly in business.

But I have observed that the Vietnam veterans are now getting settled; they are becoming successful and happy with themselves, and I believe that in their hearts they have a score to settle. The veterans are the people who acted like men and accepted what life asked of them. If you remember, it was the dissenter who was celebrated in the '60s and early '70s, and perhaps this country needed that then, but internal dissenters don't build great nations. If this country is to go on and become the world leader that it has the potential to be, it will be done by those who appreciate this country and who know how to accept whatever assignment falls to them and make the best of it.

The Vietnam veteran is getting his act together now, and he and his supporters will have a lot to say in the years to come. As for myself, if the fates permit, one day, at the right time and in the right place, I shall spit in Jane Fonda's face.

FRED G. ALDERMAN, DENVER, COLORADO

Upon my return from Vietnam in March 1969, I was assigned to duty in Detroit, Michigan. I was given the duty of notifying and providing assistance to the next-of-kin whose loved ones were killed in Vietnam. This job required special care and sensitivity to assist people who had lost someone they cared for.

While walking through a local shopping mall I was spat upon by other Americans. It was quite a shock to have people so hostile toward me. I felt rejected by my country, and still do. The same country that I was willing to die for, if necessary.

To the American people: please, for my sake and for the sake of other Vietnam veterans, understand that we want to come home. Unfortunately for many, the horrors of the war will last a lifetime. And also to the American people: thank you for listening to our stories.

Back in the preface of this book, I mentioned that I was going to point out a few things that you would not normally expect to find in an introduction. I also said that there would be several junctures where I would step in for just a few words. This fits into both of those categories.

By now, you may be thinking about the similarity of many of these letters, and the parallels of the experiences the veterans are citing. Please . . . stay with them. I have been through all the letters in the book, and I am aware that at this point there is a good chance that you're wondering

*whether this apparent sameness warrants your going ahead.
Trust me if you will—as the story unfolds, you will see and
feel the changing tapestry of emotions and narrative flow.*

*At this point in the book, it seems important for us to rec-
ognize that this seeming repetition of the spitting scenarios
has a very real significance. The stereotype of the feelings of
Vietnam veterans when they returned home is that they were
filled with anger and rage. Certainly that is there—but as you
have seen in the letters you have read so far, the dominant
theme is that of pain and hurt. For years—literally or symbolically—there has been an instinct on the part of many
veterans almost to hide when it comes to talking about the
specific details of their homecoming experiences, as if the
shame is somehow theirs. So, yes, up to this page many of
the letters may seem like echoes of each other. That says
something, at least to me—it says that these things really did
take place, and that only now are they beginning to be discussed.*

*Again, I suppose it's unusual to step in and speak to you
like this. But, in a lot of ways, for reasons you are becoming
aware of, this is an unusual tale. It's probably presumptuous
to make this suggestion to you, but I will anyway: Stick
around.*

JAMES A. BUSK, BISBEE, ARIZONA

I was an M.P. in Vietnam and in July 1971, in order to get
an "early out" of about 20 days, I was escorting a group of
prisoners back to the States. This was a very special prison
shipment, in that all six of the prisoners were Americans who
had been convicted of murdering other Americans in Vietnam. We were escorting them to Fort Leavenworth, Kansas.
As a buck sergeant, I was the lowest-ranking of the eight

escorts. There was an Officer in Charge, a senior officer, and six of us handcuffed to the six prisoners.

The man I was handcuffed to could have easily been mistaken for a pro halfback. Physically impressive, he was quiet, thoughtful, and polite. He had shot and killed his commanding officer and first sergeant, and crippled the officer of the day, because they had turned off his tape player during a perimeter blackout.

Once the plane was airborne, the handcuffs could come off, but at all other times we were handcuffed to the prisoners. This was for a total of 67 hours. We flew to Japan, then Alaska, then Travis Air Force Base where we spent a night. We then went to the San Francisco airport to take a commercial flight to Kansas.

It was while going through the San Francisco airport that the incident happened. There was a large group of protesters in the airport—they chanted slogans, waved signs, and screamed at us for being "pigs." Several spat at us, jumping out of the crowd to spit and then jumping back into the crowd. I don't believe I have ever felt such impotent rage in my entire life. One sandaled foot got close enough and I stomped on it as hard as I could.

I certainly understood the opposition to the war, though I felt it was rather ill-informed at the time. But I had been drafted, had tried to do my job and keep my nose clean, and I could not understand the personal antipathy of those protesters. They sided with our prisoners and against us, simply because we represented authority. Their total ignorance of the facts of the situation and their misdirected passion were perhaps excusable, but at the time, I think I would have gladly blown them away.

How often, and to whom, similar incidents may have happened, I don't know. But what happened to me remains the single most unpleasant memory I have of the war and my service in the Army.

J.E. GARLITZ, MANITOU SPRINGS, COLORADO

Yes, I was spat upon, however, not at an airport.

The event occurred in the late summer of 1969 on the four-lane drive which goes along the Chesapeake Bay in Norfolk, Virginia. I had returned from my second combat tour aboard the USS Kitty Hawk where I flew high-speed reconnaissance over North Vietnam. I had been reassigned to the Naval Safety Center in Norfolk, and lived in Virginia Beach.

Each day I drove to and from work in my convertible with the top down; I was always in uniform. My route took me along the above-mentioned drive which connects directly with Shore Drive in Virginia Beach. A portion of the drive in Norfolk went through what I would describe as a "hippie" hangout and residential area. Generally in the afternoon, there were several hippies congregated at a particular point where there was a red light. On a couple of occasions when I stopped at the red light, there were glares and anti-war language which I ignored.

On the afternoon of the incident, several of the hippies approached the car and spat on me as they cursed me and called me names. The light changed almost immediately, and I proceeded without further incident. Thereafter, during the warm weather when I knew they would be present, I used my other automobile—not the convertible. I could see no advantage in perpetuating the isolated incident.

In summary, I concur with the Navy pilot in the movie "Hanoi Hilton" who in effect stated that he did not go to Vietnam to serve his country—he was sent to serve his government. Being spat upon was merely a gesture of the reality to come.

BARRY W. STREETER, COLUMBIA, SOUTH CAROLINA

Please excuse the unpolished nature of this letter—I am writing on the spur of the moment, during a break from studying for a professional exam.

I returned from Vietnam in November 1971 on emergency orders after eleven months in country. It would have been on or around the 18th, but given the frantic nature of my trip home and the intervening years, I could be off by three days either way.

My flight came in at San Francisco airport and I was spat upon three times: by "hippies," by a man in a leisure suit, and by a sweet little old lady who informed me I was an "Army asshole." I was minding my own business, having just cleared the passenger aisle and heading for my luggage en route to Oakland Airport in order to make an eastbound flight.

I don't know that the young people in jeans were hippies—please don't assume that the only people who took out frustrations with government policy on individual soldiers were members of the counterculture.

The incident didn't scar my psyche or embitter me, but it did crystallize the Vietnam experience for me. I was only a few years older then than the majority of the dozen or so people who hurled insults and spit, but we were worlds apart in political views, manners, and dignity. The spit only soiled my uniform, but their cowardice and hatred marked them for life.

As you seem interested in fables, let me tell you of a greater injustice perpetrated on the young people who served, perhaps, in spite of their own political beliefs.

To my knowledge, every American unit in Vietnam supported orphanages, schools, clinics, and hospitals in that country. The money came from the pockets of the GIs, and the means of construction was by virtue of young soldiers giving up the only "day off" they had gotten in months, to lay bricks, dig wells, and scrounge furniture, clothing, and school books for the unfortunate children of the war.

Most journalists wrote about the conflict from the safety of the Carousel bar in Saigon, from second- and third-hand reports. Relatively few went into the countryside like Tim Page (photographer). Saigon bureau, clearinghouse for wire services, just didn't clear stories that "were just of human interest, and not about the war."

If people—a very small minority—spit at returning GIs, the press must bear some responsibility for shaping public opinion. Vietnam was more than a combat area, it was a people living in fear, with little or no hope for a brighter future. Vietnam was the stage for some of the most selfless acts of human compassion.

Perhaps others who, when they got home, were greeted with disdain, were scarred by the experience, but for myself I can only pity those who let others shape their opinions.

LARRY MAY, LIMA, OHIO

I am 53 years old and to date have never answered a column or written a letter to a newspaper. I have never felt the need to do so on any subject, until today. My oldest daughter read me your column after supper today, and I felt compelled to answer.

I spent two tours in Vietnam and returned both times to not a very good homecoming either time by the public in general. I received catcalls from a distance and putdowns like "baby killer," etc. I had people spit on the ground near me. I don't know if it counts. No one ever actually spit on my chest.

Having to wait to be served in a café, or being the last person helped at an airline ticket desk—we all, I am sure, felt very out of place in our uniforms once we got back to the United States. Us lifers wore the uniform anyway as sort of a defiance of those that we called hippies at the time—a hippie, we thought, being anyone with hair longer than the military and in less than casual dress.

To be fair, not all Americans made us feel bad. But very few of us were ever just told, "Welcome home, Marine, it's good to have you back."

I have gone on long enough, I'm sure. I didn't go into a lot of detail, but I hope you understand what I am telling you. I haven't typed a letter in 14 years.

Lawrence F. Gervais, Downers Grove, Illinois

Upon my return from Vietnam and my departure from the Army, I resumed my studies at Southern Illinois University in Carbondale, Illinois. This was in 1971. That summer I took an intensified language course at the Center for Southeast Asia Studies. The course was in Vietnamese. It was common knowledge on campus that many vets took this course.

On leaving class one day, the 15 of us that were enrolled in the course were met by a group (larger than us) of local demonstrators. They shouted the usual stuff—baby killers, etc.—and a couple of them started spitting. I got hit with the spit.

Before most of us could react, one of our guys rushed forward and punched one of the spitters right in the face. The demonstrator went down. The rest of the demonstrators fled. End of demonstration.

In retrospect, this demonstration was not unlike a firefight. It was a short, quick confrontation.

After leaving the service and resuming my studies, graduating and taking a job as a teacher, I have had the chance to meet and talk with many of those who demonstrated, either while I was serving, or before or after. The bottom line on most of those people is they were afraid to go because they were afraid they would be killed. They have said so. I can say I felt the same way. But I went.

JOHN E. MUNNELLY, PORTAGE, MICHIGAN

I was spat upon at National Airport in Washington in the fall of 1970. Witnesses to the incident were my mother and father.

At the time I was assigned to the Pentagon in the office of the Chief of Staff, U.S. Army.

I served in Vietnam 1966–1967 and went back for a second tour of duty in Cambodia 1972–1973. As a career military officer I also served in Korea 1950–1951.

The incident—spitting on an officer in uniform—occurred while I was seeing my parents off to return to their home in Chicago after a visit in Washington with me and my family. I was attired in uniform. The spitter spit at my back. My mother and father were shocked, but did not tell me at the time because of concern for me and what I might do. They told me after the perpetrator had left the scene and I confirmed the fact by finding fresh spit on my back.

I served on active duty in the U.S. Army from June 1947 to April 1980, retiring as a colonel.

ROBERT J. ARVIN, JR., CHICAGO, ILLINOIS

When I returned to the United States from a tour of duty during August of 1968, I did not encounter any individuals in the airport who spat at me.

But then I was assigned to the Marine Recruiting Office in Elgin, Illinois. I attended night classes at Elgin Community College, and the students and faculty knew I was in the service. I talked to parents about their sons and daughters joining the service, and was invited to social functions by various organizations within the community. Several times there were demonstrations outside the recruiting offices but in general the demonstrators were friendly. A couple of times individuals got into the offices and stood on top of desks and read articles about the "illegal war in Vietnam," but caused no damage.

All was not rosy, though. I cannot speak for other recruiters, but myself and other recruiters in the Elgin office dreaded making visits to the high schools throughout the Elgin area, including Carpentersville and Lake Park. It was there that we were spit at, had eggs thrown at us and our vehicles, and called names at school assemblies. A grown man does not retaliate against 15-, 16-, and 17-year-old children. They were only repeating what they heard and were taught by their teachers. Don't get me wrong—I am not talking about all teachers, but the few who ran off to college and became teachers to keep from being sent to Vietnam, and who brought their college attitudes into the high schools. I took insults that no man should have to take, but it passed as has the war.

Time goes forth and so must we. I now have 26 years' service with the Marine Corps and am looking toward my retirement. I have no regrets but I hope that those students in the late '60s and early '70s have learned the truth and feel as deeply about their country as I do.

JEANNE COLSON, BYRON, CALIFORNIA

I am a recent widow of a Vietnam veteran. My husband was killed in an automobile accident in April 1987. In January of 1968 he was spat upon by "hippies" at the San Francisco airport upon his return from Vietnam.

In your article you spoke of hippies as not being the most macho people in the world, and said that the image of them approaching and spitting on a "burly Green Beret in full uniform" was unthinkable. Do you really think that "burly Green Berets" were the only ones that went to that hell hole? My husband was neither burly nor an infamous Green Beret (not to diminish their contribution). Bradley was a grunt . . . a high school graduate who got drafted because he didn't go to college. I can still see him reluctantly entering the Oakland induction center—five feet ten, 140 pounds in his shorts, and it was "Count off."

At a family gathering he attempted to defend his decision not to flee to Canada. And he was attacked verbally for defending himself. It got ugly.

Oh, by the way . . . after he was spat upon at the San Francisco airport, he finally convinced a cabdriver to drive him home to Oakland. The cabbies didn't want to have anything to do with him; he was lectured the whole way. The driver said if all the boys had refused to go, there would be no war.

In retrospect, Brad was proud to serve his country, and he knew he was lucky to come home at all. But he seldom shared stories.

DENNIS JACKSON, LOVELAND, COLORADO

I was spit on while in full dress uniform in Memphis, Tennessee. This happened before I went to Vietnam—not after.

I served in the Marine Corps from August 1969 to June 1973. Boy, was I proud of that uniform, but I guess besides my family and a few close friends, that was it. Everywhere I went I felt disapproval when people saw my uniform. When a man was in uniform on an airplane flight—this happened regularly—every seat would fill up but no one would sit in a vacant seat next to a serviceman unless it was the last seat.

I was sent to Memphis in December 1969. What a shock! We were treated awful. At 18 years of age, I felt like I would have been treated better if I were a long-haired, dope-smokin' "good ole boy." But I enlisted, so here I was questioning myself and my uniform. All the hippie types were always claiming "Peace, love, etc."—but only to those *not* in uniform. Here I was, roughly the same age (maybe younger) than some of the protester types. And I was hated. I've never quite resolved it in my mind to this day. I just keep it buried with all the other rot in my mind (from my experiences).

Anyway, the people who spit on me were in a passing car—didn't have the courage to walk up to me to spit. This was in February or March of 1970. The guy who spit was probably the same age I was. Most people would've shrugged it off as a youthful prank, but I couldn't, because I was trying to be proud, to justify my misery.

It seemed to set the tone for my entire hitch. After Kent State had taken place "we" all really were questioning ourselves, but by then we had grown quite rebellious toward the protesters. If you are treated like an animal everywhere you go, you soon figure "What the heck, maybe I am an animal, maybe I'll be an animal. Yep! Shoulda shot more of those protesters." Identity crisis time.

You want to do right. You think you're doing right. Instead of dropping out you're serving your country, but public opinion says you're scum. So there I was in Marine dress greens with spit running down my arm.

I didn't go to Vietnam until June 1972. A little late, but contrary to popular belief it was still there. It makes you feel real odd. A freshly made-out will, tearful good-byes with family and friends, and people booing us and throwing eggs. And do I have mixed-up feelings about that period of time? You bet. Can't imagine why.

ERNEST R. HUERTA, CHICAGO, ILLINOIS

I was spit at, while in uniform, in Chicago. The assault was unprovoked and I had no prior contact with my antagonist.

The incident occurred on Rush Street in early April, 1970. It was my last night at home. The month before I had been granted a 30-day leave from the Americal Division for extending my tour of duty in Vietnam for six months. My buddy Ron, himself a Vietnam veteran, was with me. Ron had been discharged from the Army in 1968, and wanted to treat me to my last night on the town. He insisted that I wear my uniform.

While walking on Rush Street, just talking and taking in the sights, we were approached by two young men (18–20 years old). I was all of 24 at the time. The shorter of the two began shouting, "Baby killer, woman killer" at me. He then spit at me, but his aim was off and he missed.

Thoughts ran through my mind, bad thoughts. Concluding that I hadn't come all this way to beat up on Americans, I put my base instincts behind me and moved around the jerk. Besides, I was in uniform and brawlings on the public way would degrade that uniform.

My buddy Ron, no longer being in the service, held no such sentiments. He wanted a piece of the spitter's ass and went after him. I pulled him away and the spitter's partner did likewise. We departed Rush Street for more quiet surroundings.

Less than a week after this incident I reported back to my unit at Hawk Hill in Vietnam. Hawk Hill was a large base that drew an awful lot of mortar and artillery rocket fire. As a consequence, everyone lived in underground bunkers. The area was hot and humid and two-inch-long beetles would bite the hell out of you at night while you tried (laugh) to sleep. But when I got back there I actually felt happy.

BILL KEMPNER, SAN FRANCISCO, CALIFORNIA

I was an 18-year-old West Point cadet from the New York
metropolitan area. I was away from West Point to see Army
play Manhattan College in the NIT basketball tournament at
Madison Square Garden, then to slip home for a few hours.

While I was walking to Penn Station and the Long Island
Railroad, happy to be free for a few hours, a young woman
in the lobby saw me in uniform (again—I was 18 years old)
and proceeded to come over to me, calling me a "fucking
warmonger." ("Fuck" was a big word in those days.) And
she spat on my uniform.

I came from a home where women weren't for hitting, and
I just looked at her, wiped my blouse with a handkerchief,
and said, "If you were a man, I'd kill you." I walked away.
She laughed and laughed. It burned me for years.

It wasn't until "An Officer and a Gentleman" and "Top
Gun" came out that we came back in vogue, but people were
uncomfortable around a uniform for years.

JOHN J. QUIRK, SOUTH HOLLAND, ILLINOIS

After serving in Vietnam from June of '66 to June of '67,
I returned to the States to a wonderful reception.

It was the first week in June. I landed at Travis Air Force
Base in California, went to the Oakland Army Terminal, and
was cleared to go home for 30 days' leave. I bought a ticket
for a flight to Chicago that was scheduled to depart at approximately 4 p.m. Pacific Time. As I walked through the
terminal, I noticed several long-haired people but thought
nothing of it until I was approached by a young couple who
stopped me and asked if I were returning from Nam.

As they were smiling and seemed friendly, I said yes. With
that they both started calling me names—Baby Killer and

Fascist Dog, among others—before the girl spat at me as her friend shoved me.

An airport security guard saw this and came over to help me. The couple just walked away and melted into the crowd. The security officer calmed me down and stayed with me until my flight left.

This may not seem so bad but when you are a wide-eyed 20-year-old who is soon to learn that he was lied to by his country and made fun of by a lot of people who would never serve in any way, it hurts.

I have never told a soul what I tell you here but it is true and I will swear on it.

Two of the last three letters—the letter from John Quirk, which you have just read, and the letter from Ernest Huerta— point out themes that keep appearing not only in many of the letters that are included here in the book, but also in letters I received that did not end up being printed here.

What Mr. Quirk said—"I have never told a soul"—is a surprisingly common response from the veterans. It harkens back to the idea that somehow they felt ashamed for having been spat upon. That seems almost incredible now, but think about it: young men, returning from long months halfway around the world, hoping to see welcoming faces—and some- one spits on them. They did not have the benefit of twenty years' hindsight; in some cases they did not even have the benefit of five minutes' hindsight. Combine their youth, their exhaustion, and their confusion, and perhaps it is not all that difficult to understand how some of them have had fleeting thoughts, however deeply buried, that in some way they may have been partially at fault for enraging their fellow citizens. I suppose when you feel that way, you tend not to share it with too many people.

And Mr. Huerta's comment that he "actually felt happy"

to go back to Vietnam after a month's leave in the U.S.—it
seems unbelievable. But that theme, too, keeps popping up.
And when you put it in context, is it any wonder? It must not
have taken too many of these ugly Stateside experiences to
convince some soldiers that, in a way they undoubtedly never
expected, Vietnam felt strangely like home. At least the other
Americans in Vietnam did not spit at them and revile them.

JOHN W. WAID, WESTMINSTER, COLORADO

I was sent to Vietnam by the United States Air Force in 1968. I was 19 years old when I arrived, and 40 when I left one year later. That was in March of 1969. I arrived at Los Angeles International Airport at approximately 10 p.m. (I don't remember the exact date). Needless to say, I was happy and excited to be back in the ''real world.'' As I started walking to the taxi stand, all I could think of was how lucky I was to be home.

On my way to the taxis, I passed two young women in the waiting area. One of these young women approached me and, in a low voice, called me a ''baby killer'' and spat on my ribbons. I was in uniform and wearing the Vietnamese Service Medal, the Vietnamese Campaign Medal, an Air Force Commendation Medal, and the Purple Heart.

I was stunned and unable to respond. After a few seconds, she walked away. My reaction was to just get away from there as soon as possible. I don't even know if there were other people there who saw it happen. All I wanted to do was to get away from there as quickly as I could.

At the time I was six feet tall and weighed 180 pounds. I was raised not to hit a female, and I reacted accordingly. Would I have done the same thing if it had been a male? I don't know. I was so shocked I don't know what I would have done in that case.

I have never talked to anyone about this incident and I have no idea if other vets experienced the same thing upon their arrival home. Sometimes things happen and you can't react. Hours, or even days, later, you wish that you could relive the incident so that you could do what you have had time to think about. The snappy retort to the stupid question, whatever. The moment has passed and you can't change what has happened.

As I stated above, I don't know about other vets. I only know what happened to me.

TYLER SWEET, EAGLE RIVER, ALASKA

Though my memory concerning the days immediately after my return from Vietnam is somewhat foggy, I would like to confirm what happened to me upon returning from "country."

I returned in November of 1968, landing at Travis Air Force Base, California. I still had blood on my fatigues from a fellow soldier who had fallen on a bottle in a rice paddy the day before. (I was an Army medic.) At one point, we were taken on a bus through a main gate on the base. Outside this gate, a half dozen or more protesters screamed and spit at us. I do not remember anything at all for the next two weeks. I can only account for this loss of memory by attributing it to shock.

I would like to add that most of the guys I know have fully recovered from the trauma of Vietnam, but none of us will forget. There are those (as with any war) who will never rebound; but for most of us, wounds turn to scars and scars become accepted.

MICHAEL PROCTOR, COLORADO SPRINGS, COLORADO

Yes, I was jeered at and spit on upon my return from my first tour in Vietnam. It wasn't a ''hippie,'' but a well groomed little old lady in white slacks and a burgundy jacket. She looked like someone's grandmother. I was in uniform waiting for my flight from San Francisco to Philadelphia. I was a major then. She came out of nowhere, called me a baby killer, spit in my face and tried to hit me with her purse. The police moved her away and suggested I not press charges and delay my return home. Upon arriving at Travis from my second tour in Nam I changed clothes and blended in with the rest of the real world. Some homecoming. It was my immediate family that greeted me with ''Welcome home, Dad, thanks, and we love you.''

GUY H. KENNEDY, JR., SAN JOSE, CALIFORNIA

In mid-November 1966, approximately two days before Thanksgiving, I was en route from Da Nang to my parents' home in Michigan. I had hitched military airlift rides to Travis Air Force Base, California, where I took the bus to San Francisco International Airport. As I left the bus there, in my uniform of First Class Petty Officer, United States Navy, with wings of gold and wearing my treasured black beret earned on river patrol boats, I was accosted by several individuals. Whether or not they were ''hippies'' I cannot witness. But one young man did spit in my direction, and it did land on my trousers and shoes.

In early October, 1968, at Washington National Airport, in one of the snack concessions, when I refused to discuss ''the war'' with a group of what I took to be college students, salt was poured on my food, in excess, and I was spit at and called names as the parties hurriedly departed.

I am six feet tall, about 220, black, and in good health.

The latter incident occurred while I was in the uniform of Chief Petty Officer, United States Navy.

I did not retaliate either time, due to training, shock, and extreme grief at the incidents. I can forgive, if they just can admit that they were wrong, not that I was right.

JOHN ALLAN WYSCARVER, HOUSTON, TEXAS

It was cold enough to freeze water almost instantly in Tacoma, Washington in mid-December 1971 as I hailed a taxi which would take me to the airport where I would board an airplane for a series of flights to Corpus Christi, Texas, where my parents would greet me with warm open arms and drive me the last leg to my boyhood home and last stop . . . the end of a four-year career in the U.S. Navy as an Airman Third Class Petty Officer.

This was also the end of a tour in Vietnam in a combat area. It had only been about 48 hours since I stepped off the military chartered Flying Tiger and kissed the ground alongside other Vietnam veterans headed home for discharge, and I hardly slept a wink rushing around trying to get all the paperwork completed and uniforms prepared for outprocessing. Left behind were buddies I would never see again, good and bad memories, hate and joy, pride and failure. I was fascinated by the beauty of a country which I'd grown up in and yet had never really stopped to look around at how magnificent she was nor what she really stood for, much less appreciate the opportunities, freedoms, and way of life in general that so many of us take for granted.

As the cab sped towards the airport, I just couldn't believe that I was actually heading home. My heart was pounding hard and fast with anticipation, unsurety, and anxiety. America and Americans somehow seemed to have changed. I couldn't put my finger on just exactly what was different, but I felt like I was an alien from another planet. People seemed less friendly, less open, and less human. They would stare at you as if you were possessed. I even thought a couple of times that I wasn't actually heading home—that I was in the "Twilight Zone," and that I would wake up and be back in Vietnam.

The cab stopped at the airport and I paid my fare. I struggled with my duffel bags and uniforms toward the ticket desk. After standing in line for a few minutes, one gentleman asked me where I was going, to which I replied, "I'm going home."

He asked me where home was, and I told him a small town in Texas. He paused for a moment, then asked, "Where were you stationed?" I informed him that I had just returned from Vietnam. The gentleman got quiet, the smile and cheer from his face became a blank appearance, and then he asked, "Did you kill anybody?" I couldn't believe that someone would ask someone who had just returned from a war zone such a stupid and personal question. I replied, "I'd rather not answer that question." He looked shocked and then said, "You guys are all alike." He walked away, looking at me occasionally as if I was going to attack him.

After getting my ticket and gate location, I gathered my bags that I didn't check and headed for the departure area. I noticed a young man about six feet tall with frizzed or bushed hair, dark glasses, sloppy blue jeans, worn sneakers, a dirty sweat shirt, and a military Marine foul-weather coat displaying military medals and sergeant stripes. I confronted the local authorities patrolling inside the terminal, informing them that I had just got back from Vietnam and I didn't appreciate the way the individual was dressed—he was wearing the Marine outergarment, and I said that it was against the law to wear a military uniform other than in the proper manner, and it was unlawful to wear the uniform if you haven't served, and once discharged you weren't supposed to wear it unless in a ceremony, and complete when done so.

I had lost a few good buddies who wore that uniform with pride, and I didn't like to see it taken so lightly.

I was quickly informed to mind my own business—I was told that maybe the young man was a Vietnam veteran too. When I told the officers that I doubted if the man was a veteran, and asked them to do something about it, one of them said, "If you don't like it, why don't you do something about it?" When I inquired as to what would happen if I did, they indicated that they would have to turn me over to Shore Patrol.

I checked in at the gate, deciding not to talk to anyone until I got home and out of uniform. Somehow I felt dirty in it and ashamed . . . yet I had no real reason for feeling this way. I sat down to wait for the flight to board. Across from me sat a lady and her child. As soon as I got situated, she looked at me, and then grabbed her child and said, "Come on, baby, we have to sit somewhere else." She moved about two aisles over.

When time finally came to board, I picked up my bags and moved toward the door which would lead to the boarding ramp. Just before I got to the door, some lady passenger looked at me and said, "You just get back?" I replied, "Yes." She responded, "Did you come from Vietnam?" Again I replied—but with hesitation—"Yes." She looked at her male companion and then looked at me and without any change in facial expression said, "Baby killer." I didn't say a word. I didn't know what to say. I felt small. I boarded the plane and took my seat.

Upon arriving at the next airport where I had to change planes, I was walking briskly toward the main lobby with my bags when I felt something wet and slimy hit the side of my neck. When I looked to my right, the same rude couple that had confronted me earlier was walking away with a look of hate on their faces, and they gave me a familiar obscene hand gesture and said, "Maggot!" I realized when I reached up to see what was on my neck that I had been spat upon. Why did these people, who I didn't even know, hate me?

Upon arrival at home, my parents were glad to see me, and told me how much they appreciated me and how proud they were of me. My dad, an ex-Navy man who saw action in the Pacific, had a bond with me that only those who serve can understand.

I spent the next thirty days just relaxing, enjoying the comforts of life which I took for granted. I visited my old schoolteachers and marveled at how small the first grade chairs were. Generally, the older generation was glad to see you, while the younger generation could care less. It came to the point where I didn't want anyone to know that I had been in the military, much less in Vietnam, for fear of being treated rudely, or of my parents being treated rudely if they were with me.

G. T. JOHNSON, BELLEVUE, NEBRASKA

Nearly twenty years have gone by, and I had almost forgotten the incident. I'll try to be brief. There really isn't much to it, actually.

I had returned to the United States on emergency leave and was on my way back to Vietnam. It was in September 1968.

I was waiting for a bus to Travis Air Force Base and my flight to Vietnam. I'd eaten and bought a newspaper. Headed to the lockers for my bag, I was stopped by four or five young girls, probably aged eighteen to twenty. They had papers of some type they were handing out to everyone around.

They kept asking me questions about the war, where was I going and so on. I tried to walk off but they got me in a circle and one grabbed my shirt at the neck. I backed away and all the buttons ripped off. Someone behind me either touched me or was going for my billfold—I felt something.

I turned around and my arm hit one of the girls as I was turning. She hollered and they all ganged me. Took my hat, got the paper, and as I was pushing through them to get away, one of them spit a mouth of water (I think) right in my chest and face.

MPs and Shore Patrol came, along with an airport security man, and they stopped it. I was told to change my clothes, to go to the waiting area, and stay away from "them" while I was there. Airport security walked them to the other end of the terminal. They were singing all the way.

One Army MP said it went on all the time. I never did learn what organization the girls belonged to. I was glad to go back to Vietnam. It wasn't safe, but at least most of the "bad guys" were men, not girls. Had the girls in the airport been men, in my frame of mind (having just lost Dad) we might have mixed it up just a bit. With my luck I'd probably end up in the slammer.

Incidentally, there were people watching all the time, and no one said anything or offered to help.

Chalk up one more reason to see combat—to preserve the right of others to spit. Ha!

JEFFREY DENTICE, GRAFTON, WISCONSIN

When I left Nam in 1968 I was on a plane loaded with caskets. I did my time in country and I did it with pride. I and my brother Nam vets took care of each other there. We knew if we wouldn't, Uncle Sam sure didn't give a damn about us, and he wouldn't take care of us.

When you went to Nam it was OJT—on-the-job training. I learned how to love, hate, fear, be compassionate, and I found out what happens when the government won't let you win. But before you know it you're on your way home—maybe.

I landed on Wake Island and then Hawaii to drop off some

caskets. Then on to California. I was glad to be alive and walking. Here I am, nineteen-years-old and back from the war already.

I hopped a bus to Los Angeles International Airport, and it was about 8 p.m. As I exited the bus I walked past some dudes in orange robes, singing and chanting some song or whatever you call it. I kept walking until I was jeered and spit at by some long-haired guys along with their girls or wives.

I didn't say anything before or after the incident. People all over just watched this happen to me and said or did nothing. I was in uniform at the time and had I not been I'm sure I could have easily hurt or killed some or all of them. But to go to prison after the hell I had just came from—that would have been a waste. I wiped the spit from my face and uniform and went inside the terminal to catch a plane home to Milwaukee.

Hey, I didn't start the war.

DR. THOMAS K. HAVERSTOCK, GENEVA, ILLINOIS

I was a newly commissioned captain in the Army Dental Corps. I received my Vietnam orders and was flown out of Travis Air Force Base on April 29, 1969. While being bussed from the San Francisco airport to Travis, I saw that a number of war protesters had gathered along the fence where the bus ran. The busload of personnel was jeered and spit at as it ran the gauntlet. The only war I had been assigned to fight was against tooth decay, not the Viet Cong.

Being older and better educated than the average Vietnam soldier helped me erase the bad feelings of the whole episode. These acts of hostility had to have torn up an eighteen-year-old flown out to fight in a foreign land. If it had not been for my occupation, I could have easily avoided the war. The physical act of spitting has little to do with the feelings one senses about the people around him. I felt this same civilian disgust toward me while flying back to the Midwest on a commercial airline while dressed in my khaki uniform.

It has made me feel great to see the public applaud Vietnam units in parades in the last several years. It is satisfying to see a fitting memorial to those who died in Vietnam. It is good to see America healing.

And the people who did the spitting? Surely they acted in groups, and at a distance. I, too, doubt that any of them would confront a Green Beret type, one-on-one, face-to-face. I even doubt that any of them would have acted alone against a mild-mannered dentist who was merely returning from the 137th Cavalry Assault Team. The false bravado of group action would have been much more in character.

DARRELL SCHULTZ, SAN DIEGO, CALIFORNIA

I was a First Class Petty Officer in the Navy. In September 1967, in the Seattle airport, I was traveling in uniform with my wife and my two sons. As we were crossing the terminal, a "hippie" going the other way spit directly in front of me. Although he did not hit me, it was very evident what he meant. With a wife and two small children, there wasn't a lot I could do about it, except swallow my pride and continue on. Needless to say, the memory of that incident is very painful, and even though I spent another eleven years in the Navy, I never again traveled in uniform except where required.

JOHN M. MCCARTHY, ROSEMONT, ILLINOIS

I am twenty-eight years old and I have a good friend named Rich "Duke" Washco, who thinks a lot of this "Vietnam vet" stuff is crock. Rich and I have worked together for the last nine years.

Rich is not the type of guy to write letters, but I believe he has an interesting story and viewpoint.

Rich was in Vietnam for a year, during 1969–1970. His group saw combat action along the Ho Chi Minh Trail, among other places. (Rich contends that his unit could have—in fact, did—shut it down with relentless attacks, but his unit was inexplicably pulled from the position.)

Rich was a three-timer; that is, he was wounded three separate times in firefights. He was a sergeant and squad leader who survived the ambushes and jungle warfare and came home. He served his country well.

When it was time for Rich to return stateside, he was airlifted to Saigon, and from there to San Francisco. The guys who flew in from Saigon were still in their battle fatigues.

In the San Francisco airport in 1970, this war veteran, wounded in action on three separate occasions, was spat upon by what he describes as a "hippie peacenik." A woman—who called him a "baby killer."

Do you know what this soldier, this squad leader, this man whose friends call him "Duke" (after John Wayne) did?

He laughed. Laughed right in this lady's face. He said, "Lady, I'm so glad to be home, I don't care what you say."

His attitude since 1970 has remained similarly well-adjusted. He is married and has four children and, as I say, I work with him.

He went to a veterans' parade last year and saw the Wall in Washington, but that's it. He isn't one of those vets that are turning up at all these pseudo-events that you see on television. Not hardly. He calls those that do "career criers."

His opinion is that once home, you file the experience. Let it go. Get on with your life. Which is exactly what he has done.

Perhaps guys like Duke are in the majority. I don't know. He said it was okay for me to write this letter.

DAVID ALVAREZ, SAN JOSE, CALIFORNIA

I apologize for taking so long to send this letter. I have a difficult time writing about things I would just as soon forget. You see, most of us still want to put the war behind us. For me it's been sixteen years, and it's a shame that ridiculous movies like "First Blood" and "Apocalypse Now" had to be made before anyone cared enough to ask questions about us and our experiences.

I was in the U.S. Navy from 1967 until 1971. During that time I experienced two spitting incidents.

The first time I was in transit from my ship to a temporary duty station. It was the fall of 1970 and I was in a Sacramento, California bus station. I was wearing my dress blue uniform with my Vietnam service ribbons, and I was carrying my sea bag over one shoulder. I was confronted by five anti-war protesters—two females and three males. They stopped to question me about my feelings about the war. I declined to comment. Suddenly one of the females began calling me a baby killer and spit on me.

Striking her would have been playing right into their hands, since I saw one of the group had a tape recorder and a camera ready to record my reaction. I'm sure they hoped I would react violently. However, I just walked away.

The second incident occurred when I returned from Vietnam in the fall of 1971. I was in my dress uniform in San Francisco airport waiting for my wife to arrive from out of state, when a guy ran up to me, called me a war monger, spit on me, and ran off into the airport crowd. I started after him, but I lost him in the crowd.

Both of these incidents have bothered me for years. Because in both instances I felt like I was in a fishbowl and everyone around me was waiting for a violent reaction which would confirm their suspicions that all returning veterans were baby killers and drug addicts.

These and other incidents made me question, to this day, why I went. And who did I really fight for? I finally realized that I fought for my country and for my own beliefs.

STEVE PETERS, LAS VEGAS, NEVADA

The only problem I encountered after returning to America from Vietnam was my brother's father-in-law giving me grief for going in the first place. But I *was* spat on—in New Zealand! The ship I was on delivered aircraft to Auckland, and there was a huge demonstration in front of the main gate. Things were thrown at us as we left the base, and yes, people were spitting on us. We also encountered a lot of townspeople who were very kind and considerate, and who also met us at the front gate after we waded through the demonstrators.

I had two tours of duty in Vietnam, and the biggest thing I encountered when I got home was apathy—or statements to the effect that I was "crazy" for going in the first place.

I am not proud of the U.S. involvement in Vietnam. What I am proud of is that my father, before he died, bragged to friends and relatives that all five of his sons went in the military of their own free will, and "No one had to come and get 'em."

No amount of apathy or insulting remarks can take that feeling of pride away from me—the pride of a father for his son!

FRANK FREHE, GLENDALE HEIGHTS, ILLINOIS

During the month of May in 1968, I took the "L" train to Chicago's Loop. I wanted to see Chicago again, and this was my first chance after spending a year in Vietnam, and a year at Great Lakes Hospital recovering from stepping on a mine.

I was on Wabash Avenue. I was in uniform and was walking with a cane. I passed a restaurant, and a waitress came out the door and said to me, "Boy, there is certainly a lot of shit in this country."

I said nothing and kept walking. She followed behind me, saying things I couldn't hear, and then I heard her spit. Fortunately she missed me. Two businessmen who overheard her remarks came to my aid and told her to leave me alone.

I cannot tell you how hurt I was. It hurt as much as the wounds I sustained.

JAMES J. QUALTERI, WESTMINSTER, COLORADO

On May 12, 1970, I was wounded in Cambodia, so I returned home during a very negative time for vets (Kent State and all). I was hit in the back, lungs, and elbow in an ambush I walked into (my fault).

I was lucky in being able to go to Fitzsimmons Hospital from Japan, being a Denver native. Fitz was really crowded—they actually had GIs in the halls for a lack of rooms.

As soon as I was able I was allowed to stay at home and come in daily for treatment. But the Army required that I also have some other duty at the hospital. My duty was to hand out medals—Purple Hearts and the like—to guys who had them coming at the hospital (not the best duty I've ever had). I was, of course, required to wear my dress uniform when I carried out this duty.

One day, while returning from the hospital, I stopped at a mall. I don't remember the exact date—sometime at the end of June or beginning of July, I think. A group of teenagers were in the mall, and when they saw me they began to yell things and spit on me.

I was in a state of shock. I had already seen an anti-war demonstration in Japan, and then again at Travis Air Force Base (in fact, the first flag I saw when getting home was Viet Cong). But this was too much. My wounds were still raw, my arm was in a cast and sling. Some guy started to yell at the boys, and they left. I have never forgotten nor forgiven the event.

It wasn't just the government that the protesters were against. During the anti-war days the soldiers were truly hated by the protesters, the public, and the media alike. Just look at some old news tapes. When I went to college, I still found that hate very much alive. The other students could never understand why I went to Vietnam. It never occurred to them that I went because *they* sent me!

TERRENCE HUTTON, CHICAGO, ILLINOIS

I returned from Vietnam in July 1966—too early to run into the sort of verbal and physical abuse that vets met in later years. I do recall, however, how angry I was then—and twenty-plus years later, still am—at the protests and abuse against those fighting the war. I guess I never will understand or accept what was said and done to those who did the fighting.

A good friend of mine was among those who were spat upon by a brave young civilian who then ran away. This incident occurred while my friend was in a wheelchair in uniform at O'Hare airport. My friend cried—more in frustration at not being able to get out of the wheelchair to go after him than anything else. He has not forgotten, I assure you. He and I did not attend the big "Welcome Home" parade last year in Chicago. It came a bit late. Yes, some of us are still angry.

Ask the spitters why they did it, and what they think of their brave acts now. I suppose that was the level of "symbolic speech" protected by the First Amendment. I hope the people who did such things have learned something in the last twenty years.

CLYDE J. KING, GALLIPOLIS, OHIO

I served three tours in Vietnam, and when I came home the first time a lady came up to me in San Francisco and said, "Welcome home, you fucking baby killer," and then spat in my face.

I stood there and wished to my God that I had the strength to turn my other cheek. I tried to explain that I was sorry she felt that way, but all the time I could feel the urge growing to hit her. She walked away and I stood there and watched little kids laughing at what she had done.

I wished at that time I could leave and go back to Vietnam. I did, less than two months later, and when I returned to Vietnam it was with a hate for America.

I don't want anyone to feel sorry for me. Just admit to me that I did something right by serving my country.

DOUGLAS H. MITCHELL, SHREVEPORT, LOUISIANA

On Valentine's Day, 1969, I waited for my wife to pick me up at the San Francisco airport. That is when I was spat upon.

Please be aware that this is the third revision of this letter because although, during the intervening years through therapy I was able to understand my anger toward those misguided souls who did the spitting, many of my brothers shut down completely at this reception, have yet to seek assistance, and remain emotionally isolated to this day. For me, therein lies the pain.

Our society must be aware of the consequences of not honoring its veterans no matter how unpopular the war. If we do not learn from our errors, are we not doomed to repeat them? Therefore I, for one, do not mind when a vet speaks of his homecoming. It makes me hope that our collective conscience is a little pricked.

Mr. Mitchell is not the first veteran whose voice you have heard, nor will he be the last, to talk about this emotional *"shutdown"* on the part of many soldiers after they were greeted so cruelly upon their return. Other veterans, and their relatives, refer to psychological *"walls"* being built up around the soldiers after coming home.

Today, with the various outreach groups and veterans' assistance programs, this idea might wash over people—might seem obvious. Today there are few Americans who are not familiar with the problems many soldiers faced when they got back to the U.S. In those days, though, the only people who really knew about such things were the veterans themselves—and how do you ask for help when the rest of the world is totally unaware of your dilemma?

It would be one thing if the shutting-down process and the emotional walls were strictly a function of the war experience in Southeast Asia. But to realize, as we do now, that, in many cases the cause for the hurt had much more to do with what happened in the United States than with what happened in Vietnam . . . the inability of the rest of us to see that back then must be something that stays inside so many veterans even today.

PAMELLA A. PETERSEN, GLENDALE HEIGHTS, ILLINOIS

I am not a vet. But my husband was attached to C Company in 1969. And up until two months ago, he has not talked of his military experiences or of his reception the day he flew into O'Hare airport. I remember the day he came home like it was yesterday, and it will be in my memories forever.

My husband's mother had undergone a serious cancer operation and it looked pretty bleak. Consulting with her physician, we decided to request the Red Cross to bring my husband home. He was notified in Vietnam of his mother's condition on approximately November 14, 1969. After no sleep and being jockeyed all over Southeast Asia for four or five days, he finally arrived at O'Hare around 5 a.m. I was there to meet him (we had been married on March 9, 1968). When he arrived at his gate, there were several ignorant college students waiting for a flight. They laughed at us, pointed at my husband, called him a dumb sucker (among other foul names), then two of them spit on the floor as we walked past.

Now you ask: "Why didn't this brave American serviceman respond?" Because he had just lived through a hellish eleven months and made it home alive! And no matter what these ignorant individuals were dishing out, all he had on his mind was that maybe his mother might just die before he could make it back.

I was never more ashamed of my fellow countrymen as I was at that moment. I looked around as we walked quickly to get his bags, hoping that the policemen, the clerks, or the other passengers in the corridor would say something to my husband to boost his morale. Instead, there was silence and whispers.

Americans have always seemed to think that the soldiers were to blame. The war was not their shame; it was the shame of the United States government. But the soldiers were the visible ones. My husband is one of the many who felt the shame and suffered in lonely silence for too many long years. But no more! The stories of my husband and others need to be told to start getting the record straight.

It is people like my husband who have always been there to protect Americans' freedom and rights. People like my husband are the American elite! They have paid the highest price for freedom. They have lost their friends, they have lost their fathers, brothers, sons, uncles. Some of them have lost their sight, some of them have lost their limbs, some of them have even lost their minds, but they still love their country. Fortunately for the rest of America, there will always be men like my husband, and his brother, and his friends. Count on it!

I wish my husband could have written this instead of me, but that's part of what we have to deal with. He doesn't trust anyone—he will never allow his walls to come down.

MIKE, STEILACOOM, WASHINGTON

I volunteered to go to Vietnam while I was in basic training. I believed it was my duty to my country, and all countries free from Communism, to help fight for their freedom. I believed that every time a country became a Communist nation, every free nation was weakened. So at nineteen years old I went off to a country I did not know about.

After I was there for a few months my values began to change. I did not believe I was there to help keep Communists from taking Vietnam, I felt that I was there to stay alive. I heard about Jane Fonda saying how wrong we were to be there. Also, Kent State in Ohio happened; young people were shot and died protesting the war I was in. I became scared to come back to the United States. I started feeling angry at my country for sending Americans into a war that I could see we could not win by the way we were going there.

I left Vietnam on September 4, 1970. I stayed three days at the Oakland base waiting for my leave orders. When I got them I went by taxi to the San Francisco airport. I was wearing my uniform and felt quite naked without my rifle, and I was not sure what to expect when I got out in public again.

I thought that I might have respect shown to me because I had my Army uniform on with my First Cavalry patch and my medals. Well, what a shock I got when a group of young people met me in front of the airport and began shouting

names at me—some being baby killer, a no-good SOB, murderer—and some of them also said that I should have been
killed for going there in the first place. Then one of them spit
in my face. I would have killed them all at that time if I had
had my weapon with me, I was so mad.

Inside I was dying from hurt and shame for my having
gone to Vietnam in the first place. I was confused at what
had happened and I prayed to God to have the plane crash
and that I could die instead of being put down for trying to
help my country and another country stay free from Communists.

When I got home all my friends seemed like little kids,
still doing what they were doing when I had left for Nam a
year before. I felt hurt over and over again as one after another of my family and friends kept asking me, "How many
VC did you kill? What's it like to kill someone?" My family
told me I was crazy and should be put away in a nuthouse.
My dad gave all of my clothes away while I was in the Nam.
My nickname I had in Nam was Crazyman, and that name
stuck with me all during my leave. When I left to go to my
next duty office, I put back in for Vietnam again with the
hopes of getting killed this time. But as you can see, I lived
and did not get killed. I am in prison now and have been in
prison for over six years now.

I am still hurting inside over the whole mess, but now I
can forgive the protesters and my friends for acting the way
they did. They did not understand that I was still acting in a
survivor's combat mode, nor that I was confused and lonely
and afraid of coming home. I love my country and I am
proud to be an American. If I could I would do my duty and
fight again for the freedom of any country that was not Communist. Maybe Vietnam was wrong, and then maybe again
it wasn't. It really does not matter now. What does matter is
for the healing to be done not only with the vets but with the
ex-protesters as well.

You can use any of this you want, except please do not use my last name for I do not wish to bring any more hurt to my family for being in prison.

LIMUS D. NEWTON, DETROIT, MICHIGAN

''Ask not what your country can do for you, but what you can do for your country'' is what I remember—always.

Growing up on John Wayne and Audie Murphy, I came to the call of my country. Being young and a black American, I felt that I owed my country, the United States of America.

I came home from Germany in my uniform, a proud American. I was on order to go to Vietnam. When I got to Detroit Metro Airport in uniform, I was spit at and called a child killer. I did not understand this. I did not run to Canada. I did not dodge the draft or protest it. I answered the call of my country. I felt that I was fighting for what was right: freedom for all.

After that incident, I always wore my uniform to the airport to get my ticket (military standby), and then I would go to the men's room to take my uniform off and put on my civilian clothes. I would never wear my uniform in public again, ever.

I was injured in Vietnam and spent eleven months in the hospital in 1971. I still have nightmares. I am still hurt, bothered, and ashamed of being a Vietnam veteran. Ashamed of answering my call to help my country in my country's need for help. Never questioning why, but ''Ask not what my country can do for me, but what I can do for my country.''

I still and always will carry this with me for as long as I live.

DOUGLAS D. DETMER, FARMINGTON, NEW MEXICO

Good Lord, it has been so many years. Late at night in mid-August 1969, I was spat upon in the San Francisco airport by a man in his early twenties. I had just returned from my tour of duty in the Republic of Vietnam, processed through the mess at the Oakland Army Depot, and was waiting at the airport for an early morning flight to my Denver home. The man who spat on me ran up to me from my left rear, spat, and turned to face me. The spittle hit me on my left shoulder and on my few military decorations about my left breast pockets. He then shouted at me that I was a "mother-fucking murderer." I was quite shocked and just stared at him, probably with a stupid look on my face.

The spitter then called me a "mother-fucking chicken-shit." He was balling up his fists when he yelled this. A cop or security guard then showed up and grabbed the man from behind. I did not see where he came from, nor do I have any notion of how much time went by between the spitting and the cop's arrival, though it could not have been too long. A pretty good struggle went on between them for a few seconds, and then two more cops showed up. All the time the man who spat on me was calling me (and, I suppose, the cops) names, indicating we lacked bravery.

Having talked to other servicemen during the remainder of my service, I found two other young men who told me that they had similar experiences, one in an airport, the other in a bus station. I have no reason to doubt them. I also related my experience that same night to the man at the San Francisco airport who was running the USO center there. He confirmed what the police had told me: that a number of similar confrontations had occurred there recently.

Like most everyone else involved in the Vietnam war, I have a theory about my experience and other similar occurrences. Opponents of the war used every means available to them to make the war effort ineffective. This was partially accomplished by usurping many of the traditional symbols of war and claiming them as their own. Among these were the two-fingered V-for-victory sign, which was claimed as a peace symbol; headlights on Memorial Day used as a call for ending the war, rather than denoting the memory of a lost loved one; utilizing old uniforms as anti-war attire, instead of proud symbols of prior service; legitimate deeds of valor being denounced as bully-like acts of murder; and the welcome-home parade replaced with what I experienced.

It is my sincere belief that our nation allowed too many of its traditional symbols to be taken away during Vietnam, and as a partial result we went through so much pain and turmoil in that war. Of course this was not the only cause for the disaster in Southeast Asia, but it was a strong contributor.

I apologize for the length of this letter—a letter that should merely have said that I was spat on and that such things really did happen—but it has been something of a catharsis for me, too. Now maybe I can sit through a Vietnam movie without getting angry at all of the misrepresentations.

MRS. ALBERT FORSTER, ST. LOUISVILLE, OHIO

My son is an Army veteran—30 months in Nam. Yes, he and several others were spit at as they passed through Port Columbus in Ohio. But not by hippies. Just dear old Columbusites. He was coming in after that Nam tour injured and a little dirty. It was not safe to wear a uniform at that time. I am proud of my son—no drugs and he does not smoke. He was not treated right. He asks for nothing—he has his Purple Heart and Bronze Star.

"I Was Never Spat Upon"

Some of the veterans whose stories appear in this section do not believe that anyone was spat upon after returning from Vietnam. Others know that it may have happened to some of their compatriots, but are able to say that it did not happen to them.

What is interesting is that their answers to the spitting question are no less compelling than the answers of the men who were spat upon. The homecoming experience was so complicated, its ramifications so unexpected, that the stories in this section carry their own kind of resonance. Different from the ones you have just read—but, in their own way, provocative and even haunting.

PATRICK J. RYAN, LA JOLLA, CALIFORNIA

I served three tours of duty in the Republic of Vietnam with the Marine Corps. Presumably I would have been a likely target of the spitters, had such events been commonplace.

I have been rather sarcastically ridiculed for my service in Vietnam by various ultra-liberal college professors, after being invited as their "guest" to speak at academic seminars on Vietnam. However, I doubt if in their wildest imaginations they ever even contemplated spitting on my uniform. Had they done so, you could be compiling statistics on maimed liberal college professors.

Oddly, the professors, much more than the students, never seemed to understand that the U.S. military is subservient to its democratic leaders. Any bitch they had about our country's participation in Vietnam should have been aimed at their congressman and not a U.S. Marine.

I'm a professor now on the faculty of the National University in San Diego. It still strikes me odd that presumably intelligent men—our academic leaders—have yet to discover the validity of George Santayana's famous quote about those who cannot remember history being doomed to repeat it.

EUGENE F. CLEARY, WARWICK, NEW YORK

No, I was not spat upon when I returned to the United States from Vietnam. What annoys me, still today, is that no one ever asked me what Vietnam was like until 10 years later. Maybe they thought they knew because they saw it on the news every day.

But what I think is that people just did not want to even think about Vietnam. "Laugh-In" was a big popular show when I returned home, and for the life of me I could not find anything funny in that show, and I do have a sense of humor. My older brother who did not go to Vietnam thought it was a riot. That was what Vietnam did to us—it aged our sense of humor.

HAL PAULK, COLUMBIA, SOUTH CAROLINA

I returned from Vietnam on three occasions—1967, 1970, and 1973—as an Army officer. My point of entry was Travis Air Force Base, and then San Francisco to Florida by air travel in uniform.

At no time was I spat on, nor was any other form of hostility shown toward me. Neither did my friends experience any type of negative reaction from the public.

JOHN F. STRIEB, SAN ANTONIO, TEXAS

I served in Vietnam for the full year of 1968, returning to the States in late December. I returned on a large cargo plane flying to Alaska and then on to Fort Dix, New Jersey. Upon our arrival we were treated by the Army to a large steak dinner—which, by the way, was my first. Somehow I got home to Seattle, Washington in uniform without getting spit on—or even seeing a hippie. I have never been criticized for my service in Vietnam, although no one seems interested in hearing about my experiences except other Vietnam veterans.

I look upon my service in the Army, including Vietnam, as a positive experience. My only regret about serving in Vietnam is that I feel a year of my life was missed; it was like I was isolated from the real world for a year—after all, I missed the first runs of "Star Trek" for one year.

I feel well adjusted and am not angry at society about Vietnam. I have a good job. By the way, this is the first time in more than 19 years that anyone has given me an opportunity to relate any experiences I had regarding Vietnam. In summary, without my other ramblings—no spit, no hippies.

KENNETH L. GUILLORY, BARKSDALE, LOUISIANA

May I share my homecoming experience with you?

I came home from Southeast Asia on August 19, 1971. I was wearing my Air Force Uniform when my plane landed at Los Angeles International Airport. I was not met by any spitting "hippies."

However, while I was standing in line at the ticket counter, there was a well-dressed gentleman behind me who asked sarcastically, "How many people did you kill over there?" I walked past him and proceeded to my destination.

Onboard the airplane, I noticed several other Vietnam vets in uniform. The stewardesses would not allow us to sit in the coach section, and insisted that we sit in the first class section. These women did not spit on us, nor did they inquire as to how many people we killed.

Each stated how happy they were that we were able to come home safely.

As for my job in Vietnam, I was a crash/rescue team member and killed no one. Instead I can happily state that I was responsible for helping to save the lives of several of our aircrew members whenever their planes came in disabled.

JOE ENO, MARTINEZ, CALIFORNIA

I flew recon out of Thailand. I was not spat on, but would like to share a short story about being at the San Francisco airport late in September 1969, about 10 or 11 at night.

I had spent two days getting out of Thailand without a change of clothing—myself and about 100 other men—and when we were reunited with our luggage in San Francisco we tossed our dirty clothing in the trash in the men's room, and later we were off to our separate waiting areas.

I was waiting for a flight to Boston. There were a few hippie-looking folks; I was seated behind them, when along come some of the Navy "raw recruits." The Navy recruits started in on the folks sitting in front of me, and looked at me for approval at the same time they spotted the ribbon and wings on my shirt. I gave them The Look—which I later found out that only combat vets can give to these recruits.

In my head I was thinking, "You should take heart—these 'hippies' want to save you. Uncle Sam only wants to waste you."

The point is my feelings and experiences were that hippies did not spit on GIs—if anything it was the other way around.

DR. GORDON L. WEBB, SHREVEPORT, LOUISIANA

I am a Vietnam veteran, having served in the U.S. Air Force from 1971 to 1975. I never met a serviceman who was spat upon, nor heard a first-person report of a serviceman being spat upon.

Open hostility—yes. Unkind comments—yes.

Many people seemed to want to express their disapproval of the war to anyone in uniform. Often it sounded like they held us responsible. But no spitting.

JOHN P. BOSSHARDT, SAN FRANCISCO, CALIFORNIA

Probably I could have been spit upon when I eventually got to the San Francisco airport in December 1968, after being flown from Vietnam to Travis Air Force Base. However, for me to be recognized as a Vietnam returnee, someone would have needed a little sophistication to recognize my status from either my unit patch, my two Vietnam service ribbons, or from my deep tan. And I could've gotten the tan in Hawaii.

RAYMOND A. CARPENTER, DENVER, COLORADO

I returned from the U.S. military service after having served for over thirty years on active duty. During that length of service, I volunteered for two tours of duty in the Republic of South Vietnam—June 1964 through June 1965, and January 1968 through January 1969. Upon my return from the first tour, I was stationed at Lowry Air Force Base, Denver, Colorado, and was an active member of the Base Speaker's Bureau, which afforded me the opportunity of appearing on local television stations and before many civic groups. My public appearances were well over 175, and accounted for audiences numbering in many thousands.

I would like to stress that I was never spat upon, nor was I ever presented with any form of hostility from people in airports or at the many appearances, some of which were made before very anti-Vietnam groups. I never observed any alleged mistreatment upon returning veterans. However, I am aware of some qualified adverse treatment extended to a few deserving cases. This would be in cases of a very few obnoxious and extremely boisterous individuals who in some cases, I felt, were all show and never any action.

JERRY GARCHEK, RACINE, WISCONSIN

At no time during the more than 18 years since my return from Vietnam was I taunted, spat upon, verbally abused, stared at, or in any way made to feel as if I were inadequate, weird, or corrupt. On the contrary, people from both sides of the ideological fence have been deferential to the point that I wish they would ask more questions than they do.

My time in Nam was spent with a line infantry company as an RTO operator. My company and squad were a mixed bag—college educated, inner-city blacks, Southerners, poor, potheads, straights . . . with one common thread holding us together: to get the hell out of Vietnam in one piece and do so without causing harm to each other. Nothing else mattered! We were close, yet I have not seen or heard from any of the men in my unit. Ultimately one's emotional well-being hinged on a support system comprised of family, friends, and God.

Having said the above it follows that coming home could be a traumatic high or a traumatic bummer. In my case adjustment or at least a return to relative normalcy occurred almost instantaneously. It had to! A job awaited courtesy of a loving wife's tenacity and an accepting community of nuns. (It is curious to note that the high school at which I taught U.S. History and Economics contained a goodly number of men teachers who had dodged the draft, and two Vietnam vets.) We got along fine and the kids benefited immensely. After I left the high school I was invited back by members of the Social Studies department to show my "Vietnam slides" and relate my "war" stories.

I might be an anomaly, but I don't think so—numerous work and personal friends share my experience. We served our country for all kinds of reasons. We returned home to family, friends, and responsibilities. We coped. We didn't expect parades. We wanted to get on with our lives. Mission accomplished!

DAVID A. WOODWORTH, EVANSTON, ILLINOIS

I graduated from Northwestern University in 1968 and was drafted in the same year. I spent 14 months in the infantry in Vietnam from March 1968 to May 1970 and was discharged on my return to the United States.

While I never encountered the negative reactions that apparently many veterans have, I was met by a great deal of ambivalence. I can remember several times either at work or social occasions when people would ask where I had been, and when I would tell them they would immediately want to talk about something else. Before I went in the service, it seemed as though everyone was going; when I returned it seemed that no one had gone. The people who had not gone didn't want to hear what was happening or even talk about the war. (When I went over, I was about 90 percent opposed to the war. I came back 99 percent opposed.)

For more than 10 years I didn't really think about my military experience and was preoccupied with getting on with my family and career. It wasn't until the early 1980s that it became "all right" to be a combat veteran. The big parade in downtown Chicago seemed to be a restoration of pride for the job we did. It was interesting that in this year's 4th of July parade in Evanston, all of the veterans' units were applauded as they went by. I had never seen that before.

I am one of those people who separated my political feelings from my duty as a citizen and thus rationalized my going to Vietnam. I still think I did the right thing. I have never really thought much about the casualties that I inflicted or really any of the results of my being there.

I don't know if I would go again. I don't know what I would do if my child were drafted to fight in such a war.

WILLIAM REYNOLDS, MARIETTA, OHIO

Having served in Vietnam in 1970 and 1971, we were warned that our reception Stateside might be less than desirable. Many of us returning home came right from the field and were in somewhat poor condition to meet the public—at least appearance-wise, if not mentally.

What hurt me the most was coming home on the flight, and I hadn't had time to change clothes (like many) and had to transfer to a civilian flight in Hawaii and no one would sit next to me until an Army nurse stationed in Hawaii and heading home came along. It was the best conversation I'd had for a year.

Departing the plane in San Francisco (they said the worst places to return home were San Francisco, Seattle, D.C., and New York) I was met with many stares but no outright hostility. Later, in civvies with long hair by military standards, I had only one problem on my return home to Ohio. I was riding cross-country (trying to blow away the memories) on a motorcycle when I was stopped by the Arizona state police, who didn't like my looks. I gave the police officer my military ID and told him I was on my way home from Nam. Everything was okay then. So you can see that appearances and acceptances were a two-way street.

JACK A. BLUMENFELD, DOTHAN, ALABAMA

When I returned from Vietnam in May 1971 I was not "spat upon" or treated in any unkind way. Also, in all the years I have been home from Vietnam, I have never been criticized for being a Vietnam veteran.

RICHARD A. ADAMS, CARY, ILLINOIS

In March 1970 I returned from a tour with the 101st Airborne Division in Vietnam.

I got off the plane in Detroit and while not hailed a hero (I wasn't one), certainly no one spat or even showed contempt toward me.

Because of the one-year tour of duty, large numbers of troops were being "recycled" daily. Most "hippies" wouldn't have had enough saliva to expectorate on even a fraction of those returning.

PAUL KAHLE, CAMPBELL, CALIFORNIA

As a veteran of 18 months' duty in Vietnam, I have frequently heard the spitting rumor.

I returned to the U.S. on a charter flight and landed at El Toro Marine Air Station south of Los Angeles. I think it's intuitively obvious that the Marines weren't allowing crowds of hippies to queue up on the landing strip or hang around the terminal to spit on returning Marines. I also tend to believe that most returning veterans returned through some military installation for processing. That would tend to eliminate a guy fresh out of the jungle being presented with mobs of spitting protesters upon arrival in the U.S.

I subsequently flew from L.A. International to San Jose for leave and then from San Jose to San Diego for assignment to my next outfit. I did this traveling in full uniform including two rows of ribbons and various other paraphernalia hanging onto my chest. I had a lot of people talk to me about the war, even to the point of argument. At no time did anyone attempt to spit on me. I am not a "burly Green Beret" type and would not by appearance have intimidated anyone into not spitting if they wanted to.

The unit I joined in San Diego was staffed largely by veterans returning from Vietnam with less than a year to serve. In talking to these guys I never ran into a single instance of spitting. In the years since, I have kept in touch with some of the guys I served with and have met additional veterans. I have never met anyone who had witnessed or been victim of "hippie spitting" or any other type of spitting or harassment.

I have to believe that the "ugly war story" is a figment of someone's imagination. At best it might be an isolated incident prompted by a heated argument.

PAUL KANT, TUCSON, ARIZONA

No, I have never been spit on. I landed at Travis Air Force Base, departed San Francisco International Airport in uniform, and no one ever said anything bad or ill to me. I returned from Vietnam in October 1969. Quite frankly I am tired of listening to the minority speaking for the majority. I think they are full of bull.

STEVEN GIST, CARDINGTON, OHIO

I served with the Marines in Vietnam from December 1966 through January 1968. When we came back to the States and were being processed, we were warned by an officer that there had been "incidents" of anti-war demonstrators giving servicemen a hard time at the Los Angeles airport. We found this hard to believe—but were wary all the same.

When we got to the airport a bunch of us headed for the first bar we saw (I wasn't old enough to buy a drink when we went over). We ordered our drinks and never paid for the first one—they just kept on coming from other patrons in the bar who knew that we just got back from Vietnam. I was treated better at the airport than I was at home.

I was asked by a woman at O'Hare in Chicago if we were killing lots of civilians—but she seemed to be sincere. And after I began to watch the evening news on TV, I could see why she might ask such a thing.

I was never spit on. I was never spat at. I never have talked to any other vet who was. Someone always claims to know someone else who was—and always at an airport. Like most other things concerning Vietnam, I think it was probably blown out of proportion. Most people really just didn't give a damn whether you were there or not, and I think most people still don't.

LESTER G. FRAZIER, DALE, TEXAS

For several years I have asked the "spitting" question to those who served in Southeast Asia. To date ALL answers have been negative, with many veterans thinking my question absurd.

As a five-tour combat veteran, I have never been spat upon nor have I ever known of a Vietnam veteran so treated. As I recall, their most frustrating treatment, at the hands of a minority of the public, was indifference.

I believe the myth has been propogated by "professional Vietnam veterans"—those attempting to gather pity from the American public by their publicized antics. These same fellows weep and gnash their teeth in front of the Vietnam Memorial for the TV cameras.

Vietnam veterans returned to the U.S. via Military Airlift Command (MAC) or contract commercial airlines. In either case, these aircraft landed exclusively at military bases. Uniforms were required apparel for the trip home. Invariably the veteran shed his uniform prior to leaving the military terminal—not to preclude "hippie confrontation," but because the uniform was dirty, perhaps tattered, and stunk of Southeast Asia.

Look at it this way: If a combat-hardened GI had been spat upon, any media coverage would have focused on the intensive-care-unit recovery progress of the spitter, not on the bruised knuckles of the spittee.

GARY HEMMI, MADISON, OHIO

Stories get blown out of proportion.

I came back to the world on August 25, 1970. The only negative thing that I can recall was waiting in the San Francisco airport for a plane back to Cleveland.

A buddy of mine was from Cleveland and we had spent

14 months and six days together in the 25th Infantry Division. We had four hours to kill before one flight left San Francisco for Cleveland. We went into the bar at the airport for a drink. We both felt like we were on Cloud Nine to be back in the world. In our dress greens and in a state of euphoria we ordered two drinks.

They refused to serve me because I was only twenty years old. We decided to go up to the restaurant upstairs in the airport and order a big dinner and drinks. They served me drinks with my dinner with no questions about age.

The welcome home I received from my family and friends was very positive. I can't recall any hostility directed toward me for being a Vietnam veteran. I didn't want a party like my parents wanted. I just wanted to get back into my civilian clothes and start living again. It was party time just getting home!

I'll never forget "circling" Cleveland and seeing the Terminal Tower. I told my buddy, "We're home, man! We made it!"

A friend picked us up at the airport and was doing 75 or 80 miles per hour on Route 71. I told him to slow it down. I wasn't back to Painesville yet and I had to get there to be home.

MIMEOGRAPHED LETTER SENT HOME FROM VIETNAM BY VARIOUS SERVICEMEN (APPARENTLY HANDED OUT BY RED CROSS VOLUNTEERS IN SOUTHEAST ASIA)

In the very near future, the undersigned _____ will once again be in your presence; dehydrated and demoralized, to take his place again as a human being with the well known form of freedom and justice for all; to engage in life, liberty, and the somewhat delayed pursuit of happiness.

In making your joyous preparations to welcome him back into organized society you should provide certain allowances for the crude environment which has been his miserable lot for the past twelve months. In other words, he might be a little Asiatic from Vietnamesitis and Overseasitis, and should be handled with care. Do not be alarmed if he is infected with all forms of rare tropical diseases. A little time in the "Land of the Big PX" will cure his maladies.

Therefore, show no alarm if he insists on carrying a weapon to the dinner table, looks around for his steel pot when offered a chair, or wakes you up in the middle of the night for guard duty. Keep cool when he pours gravy on his dessert or mixes peaches with his Seagrams VO. Pretend not to notice if he eats with his fingers instead of silverware and prefers C-rations to steak. Take it with a smile when he insists on digging up the garden to fill sandbags for the bunker he is building. Be tolerant when he takes his blanket and sheet off his bed and puts them on the floor to sleep.

Abstain from saying anything about powdered eggs, dehydrated potatoes, roast beef, Kool-Aid, or ice cream. Do not be alarmed if he should jump up from the dinner table and rush to the garbage can to wash his dishes with a toilet brush. After all, this had been his standard. Also, if it should start to rain, pay no attention to him if he pulls off his clothes, grabs a bar of soap and a towel, and runs outside to take a shower.

Never ask why the Jones' son held a higher rank than he did, and by no means mention the term "extend." Pretend not to notice if at a restaurant he calls the waitress a "numbah one girl" and uses his hat for an ashtray. He will probably keep listening for "Coming Home Soldier" by Bobby Vinton on AFVN radio. If he does, comfort him, for he is still reminiscing. Be especially watchful when he is in the presence of a woman . . . especially a beautiful woman.

Above all, keep in mind that beneath this tanned and rugged exterior there is a heart of gold (the only thing of value he has left). Treat him with kindness, tolerance, and an oc-

casional fifth of good liquor, and you will be able to reha-
bilitate that which once was the happy-go-lucky guy you knew
and loved.

Last, but by no means least, send no more mail to the
APO, fill the ice box with beer, get the civvies out of moth-
balls, fill the car with gas, and get the women and children
off the streets . . . BECAUSE THE KID IS COMING
HOME!!!

SAM MUSE, SHREVEPORT, LOUISIANA

I was in the Army from June 1965 until the first of 1967.
I flew home to Shreveport several times from the airports at
Los Angeles, San Francisco, and Oakland. As a drill ser-
geant I got a two-week break after every training station. So
I had many occasions to be in uniform at airports during this
time.

I never saw any instance of any civilian spitting on a veteran. I never experienced this myself nor have I ever talked
to any veteran who did.

MARTY RESETAR, LAS VEGAS, NEVADA

War protesters were always kept a safe distance from us at
military bases, where all combat troops arrived in the U.S.A.
Once here, we put on non-combat uniforms such as khakis
or dress blues and blended into society before going to a
commercial airport for the ride to our hometowns.

At the military bases they were too far away to spit on us.
I have never heard of a Vietnam combat veteran spat upon in
this manner.

MIKE ASHWORTH, SPRINGVILLE, ALABAMA

I was not spat on. I do not know anyone who was.
But . . .
Being twenty years old in December 1968 and returning
from 13 months of killing, bleeding, and being shot at seriously, I was denied a beer by the waitress in the San Francisco airport lounge. I was told that I had to be twenty-one
years old to drink in California. Now if that's not a kick in
the ass after being wounded twice and nearly dying, I don't
know what else could be an insult. I would have rather been
spat on . . . I think!

RICHARD G. DAVIS, ELMHURST, ILLINOIS

I cannot list the dates and number of times I was spat upon
as a Vietnam veteran. It never happened.
I served in the Marine Corps from January 1964 to December 1972. In that period of time I served two tours in
Vietnam. The first tour was a full tour in country, and the
second was split between Okinawa and Vietnam while I was
assigned to an air transport squadron.
"In country" was the term used by Marines to describe
actual duty in the country of Vietnam. Another term was
"down south." Never once, while I was in the Marines did
I hear another Marine call the country "Nam."
After my first tour in country, I was assigned to an aircraft
squadron at Cherry Point (Cheerless Point), North Carolina.
Single—desiring the normal feminine environment all Marines crave—I reenlisted for six more years with a choice of
duty station as the incentive. (Cheerless Point is known for
its detrimental effect on rational thought.)
Having been born in Chicago, and being from the Chicago
area, I reenlisted for the Marine Air Detachment, Naval Air
Station, Glenview, Illinois for a duty station with a guarantee

of 18 months on station before being eligible for reassignment to Vietnam. (What can I say about the desperation for female companionship?)

Assignment at the Marine Air Detachment was called I&I duty. That is, Inspector/Instructor for reserve personnel. My military occupational speciality was Avionics Technician. I worked on and instructed reserve Marines in the Maintenance of aircraft electronics systems.

For additional duties all the Marines at Glenview were given a set of blues—formal official uniforms for ceremonies. We were required to participate in burial details and civic parades. These details occurred whenever the family of a deceased veteran requested an honor guard for a burial ceremony, or whenever a civic organization (mostly veteran groups) desired a color guard for a parade. We were visible in the community.

Obviously, the burial details were the most difficult. It was hard to watch the families suffer through the lost dreams of a brother, son, or husband. The parents, wives, and small children of so many fine, good men. Regardless of how bright the sun shined there was always a haze of despair and sadness. I made it back twice, but I'll never forget them.

Never once at any burial ceremony did any member of the honor guard get spat upon by a relative or friend of the deceased. If anything, a civilian in attendance would approach one of the honor guard members and ask if he had served in Vietnam (most of us had), and then they would add how they would pray for each of us in the future. Never once were any of us shown disrespect.

In relation to parades, we were often called upon by veterans' groups to provide the lead color guard in a civic ceremony. These details ranged from four-man units to whole platoons. In most cases, after the parade was over we were all invited (while still in uniform) to participate in the festivities, drinking and eating freely in the cordial environment of the community.

Because I was familiar with the Chicago area, I was responsible for recreation as the Special Services NCO. Whenever we desired tickets for sporting events, I just called the stadium and requested any number of tickets. The Wrigley family was particularly generous. Never once while in attendance at any event were any of us treated badly.

After my second tour in country, I was again assigned to I&I duty at Marietta, Georgia. My experiences there, performing the same duties of burial details and parades, never caused me discomfort.

I was stationed at Glenview during the Democratic National Convention of 1968. Every Marine was restricted to the base for the duration of the convention. Each day we practiced riot control on the aircraft apron in front of the hangars. At one point, we dressed in full combat gear (without ammunition) and sat in buses all night for immediate orders for assignment to the convention area in the city.

Not only did some of us serve in Vietnam, but we almost served combat on the streets of Chicago. Vietnam war era—tell me about it!

Today when I see longhaired Vietnam veterans claim how badly they have been treated by our country, I can only say (using a '60s cliche): Get a haircut and get a job. The Vietnam veteran has received all the benefits other American combat veterans received. When the longhaired Vietnam veterans cry about all the injustice they've been exposed to, I turn away. Most of those veterans were social malcontents before joining the service, they caused nothing but trouble while in the service, and they're still bellyaching.

I haven't seen any of the Vietnam movies, nor read any of the Vietnam books, and I don't intend to. If anything is to be learned from Vietnam, it is this: War—all war—is stupid!

Where was I when Chicago had the big parade for the

Vietnam vets? The same place as most of my fellow veterans—at work.

DARRELL P. BENTON, COPPERAS COVE, TEXAS

In reference to whether any Vietnam veterans have been spat upon, this probably is one of the biggest myths around.

I, too, am a Vietnam veteran and I made two trips to Vietnam and I never saw a display of hippies spitting on anyone. Of course, I am six foot one inches and weigh 200 pounds, so not too many people would mess with me.

Maybe some incident did happen, and over a period of time things got blown out of proportion.

Supposedly there was a picture of Ann-Margret, I believe, that was passed around by the troops. I believe that she was wearing some skin-tight leotards while on a USO tour. The troops believed that she was naked. I have heard reports that the troops of the Vietnam era were smarter and better educated than their World War II and Korean War counterparts, but sometimes I wonder.

Maybe the news media had something to do with the spitting-incident stories. The troops see the demonstrations and even see the riots at the 1968 Democratic National Convention—with a little bit of imagination, they can come up with an incident.

People in the airport talked to me, but they seemed more interested in Vietnamese women. I got the impression that they thought Vietnamese women were all whores. I chalked this up to total ignorance.

The bottom line to all of this is that people will believe what they want to believe.

RICHARD D. KRUEGER, LOS ANGELES, CALIFORNIA

The stories about returning Vietnam veterans being spat upon after returning to the continental United States are pure, unadulterated balderdash!

Except for air-evac'd wounded, all Vietnam veterans flew directly into military bases on the West Coast—primarily Travis Air Force Base (San Francisco) and McChord Air Force Base (Tacoma, Washington), where they were outprocessed and on their way home in about 24 hours or less. There were no hippies or war protesters waiting in a military air terminal.

I am a retired master sergeant, U.S. Air Force. I've met hundreds of Vietnam veterans in my line of work (national service officer, Disabled American Veterans), and I have NEVER met one veteran who says he was spat upon. True, most returned to the States without fanfare . . . but the stories of their being spat upon are false. Any spitter would have ended up spitting out his/her teeth had such an incident occurred.

If you're feeling confused right now, you're not alone—that's how I felt when I first read the letters. By their sheer number and devotion to detail, there can be no doubt that the letters in the first section of this book established beyond question that the spitting incidents did happen.

But in this section—presented with vehemence and self-assurance that is entirely equal to that displayed by the veterans whose words appeared in the first section—is a totally opposite point of view. Mr. Krueger's letter, which you have just read, was obviously written with no doubt whatsoever in his mind . . . as are the other letters in this section. And yet, if these letter writers are correct, what does that mean about what the veterans in the first section had to say?

In these places where I have stepped briefly into the narratives, I have done my best merely to express my reactions to the letters, and not to engage in any kind of amateur psychology. I suppose a psychologist might theorize that the veterans who say there was no spitting are possibly "conflicted"—that this is their way of closing their eyes to the fact that their compatriots were treated badly while they themselves were not. But that theory makes little sense— whatever the textbook definition of "conflicted" means, the men whose letters are appearing in this section don't sound as if they're hiding any inner conflict about this at all. Many of them just don't believe it ever happened.

So if you're confused, that's understandable—even logical. The only solution seems to be to let all of the veterans have their say, and then at the end of the book to judge the sum of this perplexing, historic, human story as a whole.

DAVE SPERRY, BATAVIA, ILLINOIS

I came home in uniform in October 1970 with absolutely no problem. Earlier that same year I left Vietnam on emergency leave and 36 hours later went through O'Hare still wearing jungle fatigues and a fresh tan. The reception I got from anyone even dressed like a hippie was more like that of Moses crossing the Red Sea. They took one look and silently parted to let me through.

W. F. CUNNINGHAM III, SHERIDAN, ILLINOIS

Like the vast majority of Marines, the volition to sign my name to a Marine contract was my own. No draft board or judge forced my hands. As a matter of fact, I was seventeen-years-old and had to force my father to sign his name so I could join. I wanted to be a Marine.

Going through boot camp, etc., all training was geared

toward combat in Vietnam. Needless to say, it was different than anything they had been teaching in nigh 200 years; it was a different kind of war from the go. The only thing I knew about being a Marine, before joining, was learned in John Wayne movies. Maybe Jack Webb's "D.I." could get thrown in here.

At any rate, once my training was completed I found my-self stationed in San Diego. I was put into supply. Supply? I never knew they had such a thing. The Marines stationed there were either new recruits like myself, or Marines who had already served a tour in Vietnam. Stateside duty in the Marine Corps was not like the movies at all; it was all spit and polish. Now I could very well have stayed in San Diego and done my three years. But the action was in Southeast Asia, that's what they had initially trained me for and where I thought all Marines went. I volunteered for duty in Viet-nam, along with about 18 other Marines, half of whom had already been there once.

I arrived in Vietnam somewhere in the first week of June 1967. Once again the U.S.M.C. put me into a supply unit; I must say, I was upset with this assignment at first. But then we had our first rocket attack somewhere in July, and I quickly learned that real war was not like any John Wayne movie. I then realized my luck at being put where I was put. So don't ever confuse me with grunt-Marines. I assisted in re-outfitting enough of them to know what they were going through, and friends I'd made in training used to stop in on their way to/from R&R and couldn't believe that Marines could live like we did—which wasn't half as good as the Air Force or Navy personnel.

I made it through my nigh 13 months over there. There were rocket attacks in the middle of the night upon occasion. There were mundane patrols to be run or a few convoys to ride. Guard duty always hung low over us low-ranking Ma-rines. I was set on extending my tour for six months, and

Charlie did me a favor. I wasn't where I was supposed to be, and where I was supposed to be took a direct rocket (seven out of 10 died, one was on leave, one was in the head, one was turned into a vegetable he had so many holes in him, and me, I was out having a good time). I decided since Charlie had my Zip Code I wasn't going to stick around until he got my whole address right: I headed home. It was the middle of June, 1968, and the government gave me $135 for loss of possessions.

After the usual military delays my first port of call in the good ol' continental U.S. was San Francisco. I hooked up with about two dozen other returning Marines. All of us needed money and headed for an Air Force base close by. We got there after hours and would have had to blow a day's leave if we waited for them to open the next day. Still dressed as we were three or four days before, when we began our trek home—but looking like it had been 10 days—we headed to San Francisco airport; it was Western Union time.

You think it was usually a case of one Green Beret and one hippie? Well try two dozen raunchy-looking, grisly Marines. Hell, no one wanted to get near us. I can't really remember seeing a hippie, per se, but people did seem different-looking; however, being in California, nothing seemed out of the ordinary. Yet, people did shun us. Maybe it was the way we looked, I don't know. But people treated us differently than when I had left from southern California a year before. (Funny note: Here was a bunch of red-blooded American boys who had been dreaming of round-eyes, and yet when we voted on who was the best-looking American girl we'd seen while sitting in the airport, a Japanese girl won hands down.) So you can see, San Francisco went without much of anything happening.

Now all the Marines that I was with came from all points on the compass. We all went our separate ways; I was the only one heading for Chicago.

When I arrived at O'Hare I headed for the buses that went downtown. But before I could pay my fare a limo driver, not a taxi driver, saw me standing there with all of my gear. He beckoned me over and asked where I was going. I told him that I was going to the Palmer House so that I could get picked up by my friends from the South Side. "Well, get in, kid," he told me. I tried to tell him there was no way I could pay for his transportation. I then learned that he didn't mean to charge me, as he was going back downtown empty to pick up a fare.

Boy, did he give me the royal treatment. He opened my door for me, loaded my gear in the trunk, let me watch the TV, and even offered me a drink from the bar in the rear, where he made me sit like a real passenger. Once back downtown he opened my door like the pro he was, grabbed my gear from the trunk, and escorted me into the Palmer House. Yes, I thought, I was back home.

It took awhile for my buddies to come downtown and pick me up. I wanted to surprise my family so I had called my friends. In waiting for them to come and get me, I learned that Chicago wasn't the same city that I'd left nigh two years before.

I was standing in front of the Palmer House, thinking that my buddies would be there any minute. A little old lady walked up to me. She looked at my ribbons and marksman's badge. "What are those for, son?" she asked me. So I explained Vietnam, etc. She said to me, "Oh, you're one of THEM," and walked away shaking her head. Then I noticed how funny other people kept staring at me as they walked by. My buddies couldn't get there fast enough.

The two buddies that picked me up were Vietnam veterans, both decorated and wounded in action, so going home with them was easy. Seeing my family was even better. Then I began to get out and enjoy myself.

The girl I had when I left sent me a Dear John, so that

venue was out. But in meeting old friends and going to parties and such, I learned that the old neighborhood was, somewhat, on sides. Some guys had turned hippieish, some were straight as an arrow, some were for the war, a lot against. There were those who served, and those who didn't; and those sides just didn't mix well. It would be nigh 10 years before some of these guys would talk with one another.

So in answer to the query—no, I was never spit on by a hippie in an airport. But I did see and feel what that war did to friends and even families. Maybe the fable of a hippie spitting on a returning vet was just an easy way to dramatize the dichotomy that pervaded the American scene at the time. I don't know. But I do know one thing: At the time, with one year left to serve, I wasn't happy, nor did I feel safe, until I was once again ensconced back on a Marine base with all men who understood.

ROY JOHNSON, HIGHLAND PARK, ILLINOIS

As a Vietnam vet, I returned to the United States in California in June 1968. Got new uniforms, etc., and went to airport at San Francisco to fly home to Chicago. People were great at airport, especially the businessmen and the airline (United)—moved us to first class at no extra charge. No spit.

RICHARD F. TORREZ, TUCSON, ARIZONA

I served in the United States Air Force from August 1965 to August 1969. In 1968 I was sent to the Republic of the Philippines in lieu of going to jail, as I absolutely refused to be sent to Vietnam. I would have gladly spent the remaining 12 months of my enlistment in jail, as I was totally against the Vietnam war and the so-called leaders who perpetuated it. An understanding senior master sergeant intervened on my behalf and I ended up at Clark Air Force Base, enjoying myself thoroughly.

Most of the people I knew and talked to while serving in the Air Force felt the same way as I did. We were not about to get involved in a war that was morally, philosophically, and politically wrong. We were basically protesting the war, within the limits of the law, while giving up four years of our lives. I guess we were hippies too, we just couldn't dress the same.

I was discharged in August 1969 at Travis Air Force Base, near San Francisco. In order to fly on military rates it was necessary to wear the uniform. Not being exactly well-off, most of the guys being discharged chose to wear the uniform—Army, Air Force, etc. I took the bus to San Francisco International Airport, along with hundreds of other guys on buses. Never once did I encounter or see any form of hostility (especially spitting) from the so-called hippies, flower children, or street people. Any form of aggression to ourselves would have been handled accordingly by any one of us.

I spent a good six hours at the airport, and if anything I was amazed at the docility and openness of the "hippies." I wondered how anybody could be so laid-back.

I would venture to say that anyone who spit or got spat on during the Vietnam era is just as likely to be involved in a similar situation today for an entirely different reason. Humans do not always get along together. Man's inhumanity to man has been going on since time began.

BERNARD GREENING, SANTA CLARA, CALIFORNIA

After spending a year in Vietnam in a non-combat role (1967–1968), I got out and became a "hippie."

I joined peace marches. I joined protest walks. I lived in a commune in Berkeley. One of its projects was to give shelter to AWOL soldiers who wanted to get out of the Army.

I went to a federal prison in Arizona to visit a draft resister I had met. One San Francisco peace march had "Vets for Peace" leading it, another "GIs for Peace."

During 1967 when I was in Vietnam, there was a draft demonstration in Oakland led by a well-known anti-war activist. I wrote and told her that I hoped she and the other demonstrators were not screwed over by the police. Her mother wrote back and said she hoped I would not be screwed over by having murder, worse yet mass murder, on my conscience for the rest of my life. Could this constitute moral spitting? I still have the letter in my scrapbook.

I am a six-foot-two-inch, 210-pound Vietnam veteran. Maybe I intimidated people. I kept my hair short for a long time because I thought it was more important to argue about the war rather than hair length. I was always open about being a veteran.

I was drafted. I did not have to make a choice that I later had to defend. Perhaps I felt guilt for not having the moral courage of resisting.

ALLAN JOHNSON, NAPERVILLE, ILLINOIS

Served in Vietnam May 1969–June 1970. Third Battalion, 187th Infantry, 101st Airborne Division.

Received a warm welcome when I returned home to Carson, North Dakota after my tour of duty. Even got a few free beers from the local establishment.

North Dakota was short on hippies, but I came through Seattle and Fort Lewis, and I am not aware of any incidents from any of my Vietnam friends. Most of my friends are well-adjusted, have families, good jobs, and are doing fine. I left Vietnam and within two days was out of the service and drinking beer in a pub in Seattle with my brother.

THOMAS J. SEVERIN, GLENVIEW, ILLINOIS

The answer is no.

This includes two tours in Vietnam which required me to complete three round trips between Saigon and Chicago. These travels included stops in Japan; San Francisco; Anchorage; Honolulu; and Chicago.

All of these travels were in uniform—either tan summer-weights with appropriate ribbons, or the olive drab "jungle" fatigues.

No spitting.

DOUGLAS CALDWELL, ABILENE, TEXAS

I went to Vietnam in 1967 and came back home in 1968. I was never spat upon, either going or returning.

In fact I walked around San Francisco in December 1967 for several days in my Marine uniform, prior to going over, and nobody even said a harsh word.

Coming back from Vietnam a year later, I traveled in uniform through Los Angeles International Airport and Kennedy Airport in New York. I never saw any sort of hostile act by any "hippie."

JIM BERNIKOWICZ, GREENWOOD, INDIANA

I returned to the States twice from Vietnam—August 1967 and September 1970. My experience was not of persons spitting on me. My experience was of persons walking away from me.

I had to wait in airports for connecting flights to get home. While standing at the local watering hole people would ask me if I was returning from Nam. When I said yes, they would give me a strange look and walk away. Or while I was in uniform, some time after coming back from Nam, people would come up and ask me if I had been there. When I gave them the answer they too would walk away.

This was all too unnerving, and it did bother me, because I was serving my country and theirs, also. I never did anything that I was not proud of. I was very proud to serve my country. I would do so again if called.

The tank crews I served with, the platoons, companies, battalions, and divisions I served—I am proud of them all.

JAY ARCHIBALD, MARTINEZ, CALIFORNIA

When I came back from Vietnam in 1966, I jumped right into drugs, hippies, and skydiving. (Might as well do it all, right?) This all took place in Ann Arbor, Michigan. Many were the hippies I knew, and they were all opposed to the war. (They called it a war, I didn't. I called it a carnage machine.) After all, a war has a purpose, and Vietnam didn't. Vietnam was just a place to kill or die. No goals other than death.

When I told them I was back from Vietnam it was the "hippies" who passed me a joint and said, "Glad you made it." I remember a soft young girl putting her hand on my arm and asking me ever so gentle if I had to kill anyone. I said no, but I would have to stay alive. She nodded yes and said she would too. When I went back and visited my old friends who were rather conventional, they wanted to know how many gooks I killed. They didn't ask what I thought or felt. I haven't been back to see them.

Now I'm 45 years old and all of that time I had the whole bad thing buried safely away until a few years ago, and it all started coming back. Went through the Vietnam Veterans Outreach program and I think I have it behind me now.

Let's give credit where credit is due. If no one had ever opposed the stinking war it would still be going on. Excesses were committed on both sides both domestically and internationally. At least the "hippies" had an opinion on the situation. The silent majority stayed quiet because they were too embarrassed to say something. Their fear was someone with a flag might accuse them of being un-American. We can't have that, can we? Better let some more of our children die instead. Embarrassment is a powerful tool.

Jane Fonda cared. She knew that the battle figures were human lives and we had no business in there. But she went too far. Way too far. It will haunt her for the rest of her life. Or she could stop making videos for a minute and apologize to all veterans who served in Vietnam. It would only take a few moments. We wouldn't even have to accept. Her apology would simply take it off her shoulders, and I know it is on her shoulders. She can pretend all she wants—it's still there.

I traveled through a lot of airports in uniform and I never saw any hippies, let alone got spat upon. The hippies I knew were too poor to fly anyway. And on top of that they were too stoned to find their way out of town to get to an airport.

Mr. Archibald's letter arrived before Jane Fonda made her televised apology to Vietnam veterans, and the letter was selected for inclusion in this book before the apology. Just as the manuscript was being prepared to go to press, the ABC "20/20" program featuring Fonda's comments was broadcast.

My first inclination, after the telecast, was to leave Mr. Archibald's letter out of the book—after all, Fonda had done exactly what he had suggested—but upon reflection it seemed important for him to have his say. Perhaps Jane Fonda sensed that there were many men all around the country who shared Mr. Archibald's emotions; perhaps that was part of the reason she decided to deliver her message to them. I know this:

Had I included all the letters that mentioned Jane Fonda's name, this book would be twice as long as it is.

GEORGE FIREHAMMER, SPOTSYLVANIA, VIRGINIA

I had heard about the spitting stories. I was never spat upon or even harassed. When I returned to my hometown, I was greeted as a patriot, with an interview by our local paper replete with front page story and photo. I believe most hometown folks were supportive of the troops and our difficult mission.

The only harassment I ever received was a half-cocked remark from an uncle who asked, "What's your hang-up, George? I understand all these Vietnam combat veterans have some problem." Considering the source, I passed it off. I believe that most of us were well received, although we probably felt uncomfortable adjusting, some having guilt about surviving while many of our compatriots didn't make it.

I wish some attention would be paid to the humor, compassion, and heroism exemplified by our men in Vietnam. I could give you many such stories that would counterbalance the classic image of "Apocalypse Now," "Platoon," and "Full Metal Jacket." I remember one of my corpsmen staying up with a Vietnamese woman in her seventies who was suffering with a high temperature. We were in an ambush site near a village, and he ministered to this woman all night until her fever broke. That one didn't make headline status. I wish the American people could know what value they have in our men who served with honor and compassion.

MIKE OLENCZUK, SUNNYVALE, CALIFORNIA

I have never been spat upon because I was a soldier. I wouldn't have tolerated it then and I won't until the day I die.

Even though I have never been spat on I never felt that my country expressed thanks for what we did.

Our plane from Saigon landed around 4 o'clock in the morning. After we retrieved our baggage we took buses or taxis to Oakland Army Base for processing out or further assignments.

I took a cab with some other guys. The driver took us to the building we were told to report to. It was a very long, run-down looking building, not unlike a warehouse.

Once inside the doors you had to go down a long, wide corridor. The walk down that corridor will be with me the rest of my life. On the walls were large insignia of the units that served in Vietnam, and many signs thanking us and welcoming us home.

After stowing my gear, I had a big steak for breakfast, cooked to order. I spent the rest of the day processing out.

Other than family members, the welcome home signs at that base were the only "thank-you" that we received. They were from our own kind, guys who had been there and knew what we went through.

It is now 20 years later and everyone is jumping on the bandwagon to acknowledge the Vietnam vets. Where were these sorry sons of bitches back then?

Maybe we were ALL spat on in that way, after all.

MICHAEL A. PARKE, CHICAGO, ILLINOIS

From March 1966 to April 1967 I served in Vietnam with the 34th General Support Group, 1st Aviation Brigade, Saigon.

When I returned home, I never experienced people spitting on me or being verbally abusive. I cannot imagine any returning veteran allowing someone to spit on him and not doing something about it. I know I wouldn't have tolerated it for one instant.

I found people were more inquisitive as to what it was like in Vietnam, what I thought of the people and the country, how I felt about the war and the political implications.

And they wanted to know if I was happy to be home.

MARVIN TIEKEN JR., ETIWANDA, CALIFORNIA

I did what I thought was my moral duty for my country. I served in the U.S. Army for three years beginning in 1965. During that time I was in Vietnam from September 1966 to October 1967.

Upon my return I went through three major airports on my way home—Seattle, Washington; Dallas, Texas; and San Antonio, Texas.

You would think that someone in dress greens would draw some attention at those places. But my observation was that of being completely ignored. I do believe I could have received more attention walking along a deserted beach.

CHUCK REED, TANGIPAHOA PARISH, LOUISIANA

I am a deputy sheriff and a Vietnam combat veteran. I get a chuckle out of stories about hippies spitting on combat vets as we came through airports upon release from the Army. I changed planes in San Francisco in January 1971 after being honorably discharged from the service. I was in my dress greens with my RVN campaign ribbons and my combat infantry badge prominently displayed.

No one, hippie or otherwise, spit at me. In fact the long-hairs I saw most often had a sad look of compassion, although one or two did show some disdain. However, they apparently knew better than to spit at me, or at the other men in a variety of service uniforms I saw in the airport.

Personally, I grew long hair, joined the Vietnam Veterans Against the War, and demonstrated at the GOP convention in Miami Beach in 1972. While in the streets I was Maced from a car window; inside the car was a decorated Vietnam vet and a couple of suited federal-agent types. Thus, I got more harassment from "our side" than I did from hippies.

I am proud of the service my brothers gave in an unpopular war, because we were the Winter Soldiers who understood we had a duty despite our personal distaste for the war. I also have a pride in the Vietnam Veterans Against the War; I believe we helped end the war faster than the Nixon Administration would have liked.

The Vietnam war disproved stereotypes.

MICHAEL MERRITT, BURBANK, CALIFORNIA

I think that what we have here is a failure to communicate.

No slimy hippie (or anyone else, for that matter) is going to get away with spitting on a guy in uniform.

So why all these stories about being spat upon?

These "stories" are just an attempt to describe the feeling that a guy gets, spending 11 (or more) months in Vietnam, being traumatized in the name of American democracy, asked almost daily to be altruistic—to make sacrifices—and then return to a society dominated by selfish assholes who think that just because they've got mouths to run that when they speak they are saying something. Who take for granted the "rights" that the poor GI is paying interest on.

So what's the deal 20 years down the road?

They give a few parades so people can see the freaks and cripples march down the street. It's all a big joke, isn't it?

Limp dicks go to see "Platoon," "Full Metal Jacket," or other movies and think that they can understand the "Vietnam experience," "heal the wounds," etc. It's all a bunch of commercialized, politicized bullshit.

Hippies, and their strange ideology about "love," "peace," and "understanding" are history—they've admitted hippieism was just another "trip," and turned themselves into yuppies. Too bad the dead and the crippled can't do the same.

If people really want to understand the Vietnam experience they should start with this: There's bullshit and then there's bullshit. If a guy wants to bullshit or tell a war story to amuse his lame friends, and get a few beers in the bargain, I say rock out. He's no better or worse than the fucking liars who write these "great" war movies.

M. J. FENRICH, LEANDER, TEXAS

I would like to get my two cents' worth in. I think these stories about spitting are a lot of bull. I am a 30-year veteran and served during World War II, Korea, and Vietnam. During my military career I received nothing but respect from all civilians I came in contact with.

My Vietnam tour was from June 1968 to May 1969. I served my tour of duty at Bien Hoa Air Base. During this time my oldest son, still on active duty today in Germany with the U.S. Army, did his tour at Long Binh about seven miles from Bien Hoa. At no time have I ever heard him state that he had been spit on. From Vietnam I went directly to Berlin, Germany, for a four-year tour of duty. I had many occasions to visit East Berlin, always in uniform, where I came in contact with people of the Oriental race who were obviously from Vietnam. My Vietnam service medals were always easily recognizable by these individuals, and even they did not spit on me.

It has been my experience that people who come up with statements such as this are the same type who walk around with a chip on their shoulders just begging for trouble. Next time you see a bunch of ''Vietnam veterans'' on television walking in a parade, take a good close look at them. Most of them look like the hippies that were supposedly doing all the spitting back in the '60s.

Frankly, I don't buy it.

ROBERT A. ESCO, BIRMINGHAM, ALABAMA

I served with the Marines in Nam from August 1966 through September 1967. I was discharged January 31, 1968. I HAVE NEVER BEEN SPIT ON. However, I have been the focal point of a few practical jokes, like throwing firecrackers my way or slapping a desk with a ruler behind my back to see me ''hit the deck'' in a natural reaction to escape rifle fire. So much for the practical jokes.

I am proud to have served my country. I just wish they would have let us win. I'm sure the scars would have faded earlier. Here's to hope for the future.

R. M. GREGSON, SEATTLE, WASHINGTON

Returned from first tour in August 1966. No problems, but did not spend much time in airports, etc.

Came back from second tour in November 1969. Same results. Always had courtesy expressed. Wish I had been as humane to demonstrators at the Pentagon in 1967. That's a sore spot on my conscience (as is the Vietnam war, in retrospect).

Peace.

JIM SORENSEN, MCKINLEYVILLE, CALIFORNIA

Neither I, nor any other Vietnam vet I know, was spat upon by a hippie upon our return home. But if such incidents did happen, they probably happened at an airport. Air terminals were our first exposure to the real world upon return from Southeast Asia. Nearly all of us returned to Travis or McChord Air Force Base, and then found our way home or to our next duty station on commercial air transport. My itinerary was from Seattle to San Francisco to San Jose to Fresno.

I'm not plugging United Airlines, but I will tell you what happened to me and another GI on a United flight from San Francisco to Fresno via San Jose. The flight we were on was less than half full, but the stewardess tactfully told us the plane was short on meals in coach, and asked if we would please move into the first class section. The other soldier and I became the only first class passengers on the plane.

I will never forget this woman's kindness, because it was my welcome home to "The World" after 22 months away.

Contrast this to something which happened a couple of days later at home, a small San Joaquin Valley town near Fresno. I walked into a bar, whose owner and proprietor was a neighbor and lifelong family acquaintance. He greeted me, "Hi, Jim. Still working in the woods?" (I should explain that I was a logger before enlisting in the Army in 1966.) What a fine greeting after being gone for nearly two years, especially considering the source.

The point is, I could have dealt with spit. I had, and still have, a hell of a time dealing with the indifference I met upon coming home. I sometimes felt I should have stayed where I was. At least in Vietnam I knew the rules. I knew who cared and who didn't. I knew on whom I could depend.

No, burly members of the Green Berets would not stand and take being spat upon by hippies or anyone else. Nor would burly businessmen in Brooks Brothers suits. As a not-so-burly ex-Special Forces soldier, I can tell you we did stand for some strange stares, although we often could not understand why we were being stared at. I admit it was fascinating to stare back with set jaw, and see people suddenly find somewhere else to stare.

Being a Vietnam veteran is socially acceptable these days. The Vietnam Memorial has helped to reconcile our generation's differences, and to dull the indifference.

Last Easter, we were fortunate to have the half-scale replica of the Vietnam Memorial in our community. As part of the activities associated with the ''Moving Wall,'' we conducted field trips for school children. I worked with 11 groups of kids, ranging from kindergarten through high school. I made it a point to stress that the Wall is a memorial to the men and women whose names appear there—that I wasn't about to tell any war stories—but I would try to answer questions about Vietnam.

As you know, kids do not pay much attention to adults. So some kid asks me if I ever killed anybody. I reminded him and the rest of the class that we were all at the Memorial to honor the people whose names appear on the Wall, and that his question was not appropriate.

I got off easy. Another fellow working with the children was asked if he had ever killed any babies. His response was spontaneous: ''I was only eighteen years old when I went to Vietnam. What's your definition of a baby?''

The movies—''Platoon,'' ''Full Metal Jacket,'' ''Gardens of Stone,'' and others sure to follow—represent only their respective directors' points of view, with an eye for what sells in movie theaters. At least the latest genre is more believable than ''Rambo,'' Parts One through whatever the market will bear.

Sylvester Stallone was teaching a girls' P.E. class in France while a whole lot of us were getting shot at. Try explaining

that to a ten-year-old kid sometime, when you are coincidentally trying to explain why you don't think camouflage fatigues are appropriate school dress.

Besides, the only good war movie ever made is "The Best
Years of Our Lives."

RAYMOND DE HOYOS, LOMBARD, ILLINOIS

My arrival at O'Hare Airport from Vietnam on October
16, 1968, was completely uneventful. There were several
tired looking travelers at 10 p.m., and I was one of them.

LOUIS A. BONO, ROSELLE, ILLINOIS

When I was in Vietnam ready to process out, the stories
or rumors were that the people back in the world were calling
us baby killers.

I never saw or heard anybody call anyone a baby killer, or
did I ever see any soldier get spat upon.

Talk about "hippies"—so many soldiers in Vietnam were
stoned every day on marijuana, some opium, or speed! We
were the "hippies" getting off the planes from Vietnam!

I am one of the lucky Vietnam vets. I'm stronger than ever
and have a wife and children. The Vietnam veterans that I
run into at times ought to blow out their torch and go on with
their lives.

MICHAEL A. WERTZ, YORK, PENNSYLVANIA

The oft-repeated story of "hippies" spitting upon returning soldiers is doomed to remain a part of American folklore.

I feel I am in a better position than practically anyone to
comment on that issue, as I had three tours of duty in Vietnam in the years of the highest public protest, 1967–1970,

and, as a resident of the East Coast, I had to travel through many airports on my several journeys to and from Vietnam.

At no time did I see anyone spit upon a uniformed soldier in any major airport. True, at times there may have been some mild forms of protest in progress, but these events were not aimed directly at individuals. This was, however, a time when everybody had a strong opinion on the pros and cons of the war, and any GI making the mistake of asking for an opinion would certainly have received one.

There was, rather, a sort of truce between the returning (and outgoing) GIs and the "love children" who may have frequented the bigger airports. The two groups generally acted as though the other did not physically exist, literally just passing by without so much as a stare or even eye contact. I can recall only one incident of rudeness relating to my wearing a uniform, and that I resolved through—frankly—a mild threat to create a disturbance. I had been refused admission to an airport restaurant by the headwaiter, who felt soldiers did not quite belong in the restaurant's special atmosphere of phony European dining. But persons returning from Vietnam were not to be lightly trifled with and I was then returning from my third tour. I was seated, and eventually served a very poor-quality meal. As I was departing, I did manage to accidentally trip the offending man, and while he probably continued to discourage GIs as patrons, he probably made sure that he didn't walk past any GIs while carrying a tray of food.

The longhairs and the GIs always kept their mutually agreed space from each other, and I never witnessed any direct confrontations in my many trips. The two sides, regardless of their beliefs, had evolved a system of mutual disregard.

The social structure of the times was so strong, however, that I am sure that any GI or hippie who actually desired a confrontation could have found one, but the image of GIs having to run a path of flying saliva is totally wrong. If I didn't see it in my three trips to and from Vietnam, via our country's major airports, then I doubt like hell that there was anything more than an isolated incident or two of direct physical confrontation.

So, we're stuck with another myth, and it will remain for the same reason that other unproven bits of folklore remain . . . people want to believe it!

DICK FRANTA, LAS VEGAS, NEVADA

Of all the Vietnam vets I know, none belong to Vietnam veterans' associations. We are all gainfully employed, some of us self-employed.

As a Marine, I have returned from Vietnam twice, Korea once, and Japan three times. I have never been spat on anywhere, by anyone. I am not big and burly, but I am not an especially meek-appearing person, either.

Most of our younger people have probably seen a lot of World War II-type movies, and were probably disappointed by the lack of parades when they got back, or the lack of concern that people had for them. Korean vets didn't get the World War II-type response, either. But with most of us we knew that a one-year tour, and rotation drafts, were a better deal than being overseas for two, three, four or more years as was done in World War II. The parades then were also celebrating victory, which we haven't seen much of since.

Many of the young were hostile because they didn't (don't) understand why we were in Vietnam, and why their return wasn't celebrated. I suppose we were there for flag and mom and democracy and baseball, Chevrolets, etc. If anyone tells me we weren't I could be sorely disappointed, because then, of course, the hippies and draft card burners may have been right.

If some of the returnees tried to debate these people in the airports, it's possible there were confrontations. But they shouldn't have done that, because freedom of speech and freedom of expression are what it's all about.

JOHN NELSON, INDIANAPOLIS, INDIANA

No, I was never spat on. My friends only wanted to know two things:
1. Did I kill anyone?
2. Did I bring any grass home?
I didn't pay much attention to either question. But although I was never spat on, I was not very anxious to wear my uniform.

BUD JONES, CHICAGO, ILLINOIS

I was there two times, 24 months in all, Marine Corps pilot; when I returned each time I returned to a supportive group of friends and family.

I've never even heard a harsh word cast in my direction, let alone a spit!

Also, of all the guys I flew with—maybe more than 100 aviators in all (in my two squadrons)—everyone has made a good adjustment to the real world. No one is whine boxing around for a parade in their honor and for the most part, the Nam is in the past, where it belongs.

LARRY LARSEN, HARTFORD, MICHIGAN

A Marine, I served from December 1966 to December 1967 in the Republic of Vietnam and returned to Marine Corps Air Station El Toro via a military-chartered civilian passenger jet.

I've always thought most of the "spitting stories" belonged in the same category as the alligator-in-the-New-York-

City-sewer-system stories, the kitties blown up in micro-waves, etc.

A theory about why a newly returned soldier would not beat the crap out of a "hippie" who spat upon him: Military personnel in Vietnam were kept in the dark, as it were, about general news back home, particularly in the early years of the war. The occasional "Stars and Stripes" or service news-paper never hinted at the incredible social change that par-alleled the war. It never occurred to the combat soldier that he might be blamed for anything.

Add to that the quick transition, physically, from a war zone to the States. Most young, slightly bewildered service-men would not have the presence of mind to react to a person spitting on them on what was supposed to be a "triumphal return" home. Just a thought.

I was not spat upon.

JIM BARTON, ABILENE, TEXAS

I returned to the U.S. in October 1970 after a year in South Vietnam. It was a Braniff International 727 (I think). The plane was full of returning Vietnam vets, all in uniform, and mostly drunk on Braniff's complimentary cocktails.

Now, I can't speak for every flight that came back, but all the men on my flight had just finished at least one year of combat in a forsaken corner of the world 7,000 miles from home. We had just finished watching friends, fellow service-men, and countless Vietnamese people die all around us, in one long, miserable year.

No hippie or group of hippies would have spit on us and lived. If you can imagine a poodle snapping at a herd of pit bull dogs—it just isn't done. The only hippies we saw either tried to sell us flowers or peace signs, or they would ask for spare change and wish us a nice day.

I hope all those nice flower peddlers are having a nice day now, almost 20 years later.

JAMES FRAME, SAN FRANCISCO, CALIFORNIA

I am both a Vietnam veteran and an "ex-hippie."

Although I spent some time in airports in uniform during the summer of '68 and autumn of '69, I never encountered any spitting hippies—indeed, I was embarrassed more than once by older folks going out of their way to commend me: offering to buy me drinks, etc.

A few years after I got out of the Army, driving a taxi in San Francisco, I did spot three Marines beating up a hippie. I don't know, perhaps he made the mistake of spitting on one of them?

Anyhow, before I was drafted I had a short flirtation with the counterculture. I marched in anti-war demonstrations, etc. And although there was a lot of anti-militaristic feeling, I don't think any of my colleagues then would have picked on a soldier as representative of the war machine. We all realized then, as I do now, that the soldier is a pawn—an indoctrinated pawn, perhaps, but no more responsible for the war than the mothers and fathers who raised him.

B. J. PERRETT, METAIRIE, LOUISIANA

As a former Marine, a Vietnam combat veteran with numerous combat missions as a helicopter crew chief/gunner, as a present-day member of the Army Reserve, I do not believe the spitting stories.

I cannot tell you how many times I have commented on this to my wife, or a friend, or an associate every time the subject of Vietnam, the Vietnam veteran, or the anti-war movement comes up.

Just to get the record straight, I want to clarify the following so that there can be no misunderstanding where my loyalties lie.

1. No one is more anti-war than soldiers who have to fight the war. I certainly was no different.

2. I am proud to have been a Marine. I am proud of my service in Vietnam. I am proud to be a Vietnam veteran. If called upon again, and if need be, I would do it all again.

3. I feel that the Vietnam war had a definite purpose and that, originally, it was a good one. That purpose was to stop Communism. We did that on the battlefield. That was the war that we won. The one here at home was lost.

4. I volunteered for combat duty in Vietnam.

But . . . no . . . I never saw one "hippie," or anyone else, spit on a returning veteran.

No . . . I was never personally spat upon by anyone.

Yes . . . it is hard for me to believe that anyone short of "board certifiable" would be dumb enough or insane enough to spit on a combat veteran just out of combat. If they did, I dare say they wouldn't be alive today to talk about it. I think a close scrutiny of those individuals who claim that it happened would show that they either were not Vietnam veterans, as they claim to be, or that if they were in Vietnam, they were not combat veterans. Everyone did their job, and we needed each and every one of them. However, there is a distinct difference between running the USO club at China Beach and being a point man for a force recon patrol in the badlands.

It is good to try to clear the air about the "spitting incidences." However, there are still a lot of festering wounds that have not healed (and will never be healed) until those really responsible for the loss of the "battle" for Vietnam own up to it and quit using the Vietnam veterans as the scapegoats.

The stated purpose of this book going in was to stay away from any political analysis of the war, and to concentrate on the specific stories of what happened to the soldiers when they came home. But it's probably worth noting that even in this context—the context of the soldiers recounting their homecoming experiences—the question of the government's strategy keeps coming up. Some men are still filled with anger that they *"were not allowed to win the war"*; others feel the same rage at having had to fight that war for a government that they believe misled them about their mission and the justice of it.

It seems pretty clear to me that while, for the rest of the country, those questions may indeed seem *"political,"* to the soldiers who fought the war they are much closer to home than that. Politics always seem distant and disembodied. What happened to these men in Vietnam was anything but.

HELEN BASTA, CICERO, ILLINOIS

I told my son about the question about spitting. He doesn't like to write so I asked him if anyone ever spat at him when he came back from Vietnam. The answer was no, and he said that he didn't hear that anyone else was spat at, either. He laughed and said that he came back in his civvies. He said that he never wore his Marine uniform after he got home.

RUSSELL K. POULK, SAN ANTONIO, TEXAS

No! I was never "spit on," physically or verbally abused by anyone during the Nam fiasco. I call it a fiasco because like in Korea, we didn't keep fighting and WIN!

My last duty station in the Marine Corps was a sergeant

major of the Marine Security Guard Battalion, Henderson Hall, Arlington, Virginia. The subject of harassment by "hippies" during the Vietnam war came up several times and was thoroughly discussed. Not once did anyone state that they had been bothered by a soul. During my 28 plus years as a Marine, there were minor incidents—such as being called a bellhop and other sarcastic remarks, such as "hero," but spit on—definitely no!

JOHN C. SIMONES, MIDDLEBORO, MASSACHUSETTS

As a Vietnam combat veteran, I did not experience any overt anti-war sentiments. I must say, however, that underneath the exterior of exhilaration at going home in one piece there was a feeling of great apprehension because we had heard so many rumors of GIs being beaten, shot at, spat at, etc. When I left Oakland, California for home, I left in civilian clothes. I was welcomed home by family and friends, and three newspapers—the Middleborough Gazette, the Brockton Enterprise, and the New Bedford Standard Times—carried the story, along with excerpts from the citation of the Silver Star I received.

I went on to complete a 21-year career, and retired from the United States Army in 1981. I then went on to Bridgewater State College, graduated in May of '86, and I currently hold a teaching position at a high school located in a small town next to my own hometown.

There are a great many "professional vets" who can tell you a war story at the drop of a camouflage hat. Now, I do not want to debase anyone's service in Vietnam, but the ratio of combat support personnel to the "grunts" like myself was quite high. Some of my buddies were radio interceptors, and admitted without shame that they never heard a shot fired. Hey, they were doing an important job.

But there are many of these combat support troops whose

image projects that of the poor, downtrodden, dumped-on, no-one-understands-me vet that the war has left irreparably damaged. It seems (emphasis on seems) too that it is these vets who give out with the war stories. That last statement would no doubt raise the hackles of many. I do not apologize for it.

What I resented most about the war was how the media, especially television, leaped on the "crazed Nam vet" story line at every available opportunity. The newspapers cannot be counted among the blameless. They never failed to mention that the sniper the police caught was a Nam vet. I never saw them print that "the perpetrator was a crazed World War II vet."

Is there something positive to be said about Nam? Yes. The Memorial. If for nothing else, the number of names on that wall has given people in this country cause to reflect on just how many 56,000 is.

THOMAS O. VIEWEG, CARY, ILLINOIS

I grew up and was drafted from a WASP middle class conservative community in the heart of farm country in northern Indiana. I served in Vietnam from September 1968 to October 1969. Upon returning from my tour of duty I was outprocessed from Fort Dix and then flew from Newark (I think) to O'Hare to South Bend, Indiana.

Upon entering back into civilian life I returned a couple of times to my alma mater, Purdue University. I do recall letting people know at the university that I was a veteran of this conflict. I never even once was belittled or berated—I certainly was not spat upon—because of serving my country during those controversial times.

I do recall at times not volunteering to my colleagues and peers the fact that I did serve in the U.S. Army in Vietnam. Very few of my acquaintances and friends at that time had served in the Armed Forces. There was a feeling that if one did serve, then he wasn't intelligent or resourceful enough to avoid the draft. Most of the college graduates used other means to avoid what I felt was an obligation. There were job deferments, marriage, having children, joining the Reserves or National Guard, hopping around the country and changing one's address so as to not get the "greeting" from the draft board, and just plain picking up and going to Canada. Serving one's country at that time meant that you were in the minority.

I was in a "Welcome Home Parade" last summer, and it did many of us Vietnam veterans a world of good. It showed us that people do appreciate those of us who "sacrificed" some of our young lives. There were those of us who felt that citizenship within this country was (and is) a responsibility and not a privilege.

Those were two years of my life that I would have rather been working on my career like most of those in my chosen line of work did. But one must do what his conscience dictates. As wrong as that conflict was, it is one's obligation to serve his country. If you don't like it then express yourself through the elections and the governmental processes available.

I can proudly tell the next generation that I served and completed my obligation. And those who didn't have to live with their decision, also.

ANDREW L. NEILL, COLORADO SPRINGS, COLORADO

To start with—no, I was never spat upon in an airport by a "hippie" when I came back from Vietnam. I would like to relate several unsolicited but, I think, relevant incidents.

First, as I said, I am a Vietnam veteran. I flew helicopters in the 25th Infantry Division from September 1969 to

September 1970 while based in Cu Chi. I entered the Army because military service (not necessarily career service in the military) was just something you did in my family. My father and mother had both risen through the ranks to be first sergeants during their short periods of service in World War II. My sister enlisted in 1967 and would be a captain before leaving the service in 1971. Another reason I entered then was to minimize the interruption military service would have on my continuing studies as an architect. A career in architecture had been my goal since I was eight.

Incident 1: I announced my decision to join the Army to my architecture professor at Arizona State in May of 1968. He thought me less than wise, considering the situation in Southeast Asia and all. He went so far as to call me a masochist for not availing myself of continued draft protection through college enrollment and ROTC participation.

Incident 2: This is the significant one in my book. When I was in the early stages of helicopter flight training at Fort Wolters, Texas in early 1969, my progress was not phenomenal. I finally managed to earn the coveted distinction of soloing, but only after two evaluation flights to see if I should be booted from the program. I was the last of my flight to leave the instructors' nest to solo. My military bearing was likewise less than sterling. I was routinely gigged for a variety of deficiencies in my room, displays, and person. The natural result was that I spent the majority of my weekends restricted to post.

On one weekend, however, by sheer effort and a merciful eye from the inspector, I managed to get a pass for one day. It was probably a Sunday. Not wanting to waste this rare treat, I prepared my khakis to move out the front gate before the dream ended.

On that cool, cloudy morning on a quiet street in Mineral

Wells, Texas, a town whose economy was largely dependent on the Army's flight school there, I saw a young boy perhaps 10–12 years old. The very most appropriate thing he could conjure up to say to a soldier in uniform from across the street was: "Hey! DOGFACE!" Greetings from the conservative heartland of America.

Incident 3: This may largely explain why I was never spat upon. I came home from Vietnam around midnight at Travis Air Force Base, northeast of San Francisco. It was my plan— and I was by no means original—to shed my uniform as quickly as possible, get into some civvies, grab the quickest means to the Oakland or San Francisco airport, get the first flight to Los Angeles and my wife and eight-month-old daughter. You see, it wasn't at all cool to wear the uniform any time you didn't have to. Why, even a 10-year-old Texas boy knows that!

I took a Western Airlines flight to Los Angeles. From the L.A. terminal, I shared a cab with what could aptly be called a flower child. In stark contrast to the greeting in Mineral Wells, she asked, "Would you care for a nice organic orange?" as she offered a share of her snack.

Since each of these episodes, I have seen the public more willing to acknowledge honorable service to a nation's call. There are fewer news articles that begin, "A store was held up late last night by a Vietnam veteran . . ." It's okay to be seen in public with a military uniform, even when you don't have to wear it.

I never pursued my career as an architect, for which that profession should be eternally thankful, but I'm still flying helicopters in the Army. There have been a lot of changes. Every now and then I wonder what that boy in Texas—now a 30-year-old man—thinks about those who have served and of those who now serve. But I don't much care.

JAMES R. FREDRICK, OAK PARK, ILLINOIS

I was a light-weapons infantryman in Vietnam. I served in combat for 12 months with the Mobile Riverine Force of the Ninth Infantry Division from February 1968 to February 1969.

When I returned to the United States and started back to school at the University of Oklahoma I did not meet any hostility. Nobody spat on me. I did meet confusion, ambivalence, and—most of all—indifference. That was painful enough.

The indifference seems to be fading but the confusion and ambivalence about what I, and others like me, did, remains as strong as ever. As recently as last summer, when I informed some new acquaintances that I was a Vietnam veteran, I got a quizzical look from them and then the astonishing observation that "You don't SEEM weird." I assured them that I AM weird but it has nothing to do with Vietnam.

I know many Vietnam veterans, many of whom had or are having a much harder time than I ever had. None of them has ever told me that he was spat upon or called baby killer (the second most-repeated story). Only that he was ignored and felt abandoned and betrayed.

JAMES R. MILLIGAN, BRYAN, TEXAS

I was not spat upon personally. Nor were any troops around me so treated. If so, my reaction would have been extremely excessive.

I once saw a picture taken in Korea of three Americans riding in a Jeep with a .30 caliber machine gun mounted on it. A lieutenant was sitting in the Jeep and Koreans were spitting on the troops in that Jeep with him.

Many times I have been very thankful that I was not that

lieutenant. I would not have hesitated in using that machine gun.

TIM FURLONG, COLORADO SPRINGS, COLORADO

Memories are coming back to me—memories that I guess I have buried away for many years.

Like many, I was not physically spat upon. However, my return to the United States was not exactly like "When Johnny Comes Marching Home Again," either.

There were no cheering crowds, no hometown band, no girlfriends to meet us and greet us. It was almost like our government was ashamed of us, too. There was no time to tell parents or girlfriends of our imminent return to "the World," as we called it. The military penned us up on Okinawa until they could find some room for us on a flight back to the States.

Oh, I'm not complaining about the way the military sent us home. I came back on a flight filled with military dependents—the wives and kids of Navy and Air Force staff stationed on Okinawa. They were able to fit 12 of us Marines after we had spent five or six days on Okinawa. What the hell, I was glad just to be going home.

I returned home in June 1968. I served a full 13-month tour of duty. Standard for Marines to serve. I survived the 1968 Tet Offensive and almost 400 days with only one Purple Heart for my troubles.

But, I SURVIVED!!

And, I'm PROUD. Proud of what I did and proud of the great men I served with!

Well, anyway, here were 12 Marines put on a flight filled with what seemed to us to be some pretty spoiled and pampered kids and snooty officers' wives. They almost seemed to resent our presence on the plane.

I'm not positive but I believe that every one of us Marines

on that flight was wearing at least one Purple Heart ribbon, and I'm sure some were wearing ribbons representing an award for valor.

We landed in infamous San Francisco.

The people in customs were nice. They seemed to realize that each of us was anxious to get home. They rushed us through and then on to the civilian airport, from where we would head to our homes.

All 12 of us Marines managed to fit into two cabs and away we went to the civilian airport where we saw miniskirts and "round-eyed" girls for the first time in over a year.

None of us acted like the Marines of movie tradition. We were very quiet and subdued, even shy. When a girl caught one of us looking at her we would turn away. We kept to ourselves and were content to just watch people scurrying by. Hardly anyone seemed to notice we were there.

However, some did notice our presence and quickly made their presence known to us.

At the time this occurred, there were only five or six of us left together, as the others had been able to catch their respective flights home.

A group of young men, six to eight of them, gathered around us. They appeared to be a little older than us and considerably better fed. They were dressed in the best State-side style—dirty long hair, dirty beards, dirty flower shirts, and faded, dirty bell-bottom Levi's, all frayed at the bottom.

This fine group started to shout obscenities at us. They berated us as baby killers and murderers and many other unpleasant things.

I wanted to smash their faces in. I wanted to cause them much physical pain, equal to the pain I still feel today.

I guess we were intimidated by the situation. None of us really knew how to react.

We just stood there in our anger and our shame, never saying one word to these people.

They were the ONLY people to say anything to us, friendly or not.

I do remember thinking at the time that if I did smash their faces in, it would mean missing my flight home should the police detain us. I had waited a long, long time to get home, and these creatures were not worth missing a quick return to my mother and father.

And when I did return home, I can't possibly describe the feelings that arose. It causes tears to come now, even as I type these words. I was home, safe at last. I guess at that moment I began to bury the war, the pain, the anger, and the loss.

It really amazes me to "suddenly" find so many Vietnam veterans—many whose tales of combat and glory do not ring true. It's now popular to be a Vietnam vet and popular to sing the Vietnam vet's praises.

In 1985, the pain began to come to the surface. When Springsteen sang about being born in the U.S.A. I felt pride. Then I heard the lines in the song about Khe Sanh and the Viet Cong. The pain began.

It's not that I don't appreciate the change of heart, the belated "welcome home," but I just would rather let it lie.

Now, Hollywood is on the trail. I saw "Platoon." Many have said it was an unfair or unrealistic portrayal of Americans in Vietnam—but when has Hollywood ever been fair or realistic? As for myself, I thought the movie was as realistic as it could be given that the movie could not possibly last 10 years and almost all of the events portrayed on screen actually happened to me or to persons around me. I watched the movie (twice) and let the tears flow. The pain was with me, again.

There is much more inside that I could say, but I am starting to feel a little ashamed for carrying on so.

PAUL R. LUNSFORD, COLUMBIA, SOUTH CAROLINA

On no occasion after returning to the U.S. in October 1969 was I ever spat on—and I wore an Army uniform for 11 additional years subsequent to that time.

My movements were never restricted because of the uniform. On the contrary, I was engaged in many conversations that would otherwise never have been held were it not for the uniform. All were amicable, although there was seldom unanimity of views.

I recall being stopped on the streets of Paris in 1976 by a group of multi-national students who recognized the emblem of the 82nd Airborne Division, which I wore on my right shoulder for having served with that unit in Vietnam. They of course had heard about the unit's exploits in France in World War II, which started with the Normandy invasion.

I enjoyed the encounter and it seemed the students did, too. All of us learned a bit about the other.

BILL MOLONY, CICERO, ILLINOIS

We landed at Travis Air Force Base, California, in January 1967 and were bused to Oakland Army Base for release.

I had had enough of flying, so I traveled via train the rest of the way home.

At no time did I ever encounter any type of adverse reaction from anybody regarding my Vietnam war duty. I had layovers in the train stations in Sacramento, Denver, Chicago, and Washington, D.C. I traveled coach in full Army dress green uniform, wearing insignia that identified me as a combat infantryman.

I was assigned to Fort Bragg, North Carolina, from January to June 1967, with other Vietnam combat vets. I can recall no mention of incidents with civilians being reported by anyone else at Fort Bragg.

JOHN KELLY, CHICAGO, ILLINOIS

I was never spat on, but I saw a "real live hippie" do some spitting.

We were not Nam vets, but veterans of the Democratic Convention of 1968, where so many protesters had gathered to demonstrate against the war.

The M.P. unit I was assigned to formed a skirmish line in front of the Conrad Hilton Hotel. The young female hippies were putting flowers down the barrels of our rifles.

A young second lieutenant came up and gave us hell for permitting this to happen, and for joking with the girls.

At this time one of the girls spat right in the lieutenant's face.

The lieutenant told us to arrest her, but she melted into the crowd. We wanted to find her and give her a medal. What she did was just as good as fragging the son of a bitch.

DON YOUNGMARK, CLEARWATER, FLORIDA

I went to and returned from Vietnam three times. My route of travel was O'Hare Airport, San Francisco airport, Travis Air Force Base. I was always in military uniform. Never was I cursed, spat upon, or abused in any manner.

KEITH L. BRUMBAUGH, BOLINGBROOK, ILLINOIS

In March 1968 I returned home after serving 18 months as a military adviser in Vietnam. My tour was mostly along the Cambodian border north of Saigon. I recall as our plane landed in Los Angeles a recording was playing patriotic music as a sort of morale booster.

I assume the expected response was to let out a cheer or kiss the ground, and some did. But to tell the truth, I was just too tired and emotionally numb to acknowledge much of anything. I guess my thoughts should have been on my buddies I left behind, but at the moment my primary concern was to be able to shower, change to clean clothes, and get home as soon as possible.

As I was departing the plane, a fellow GI I had just recently met said, "Watch out when you get off. Female war protesters are coming up to soldiers, smiling, and then spitting on them. They're usually backed up by their boyfriends who try to pick a fight." I remember finding his whole story preposterous, and I internally labeled it more Army B.S. Besides, it was a late Saturday evening and I figured no one in their right minds would be spending their time hanging around an airport terminal when they could be out having a good time. But then, I had been cut off from civilization for quite a while and I had little idea what was going on in the "real world." I recall truthfully believing that the miniskirt was just some sort of obscure Paris fashion, as there was no way the masses of U.S. females would walk around in public with their butts hanging out.

As I disembarked the airplane to my surprise there were some "hippies" gathered along the hallway. However, airport security must have encountered these problems in the past, as we were conveniently buffered from their group. Some of the soldiers got involved in a brief shouting match with the protesters, but it didn't last long since the one thing none of us wanted to do was miss our bus to the base to receive new uniforms and transportation arrangements for home. I remember as we left from the airport there was another small group of demonstrators outside the gate carrying signs and yelling, but again as long as they weren't delaying my trip home, I could have cared less.

There's been much published about how and why the Vietnam vet never received a proper welcome home—no parades, no testimonial dinners. I'm sure there are some vets who feel betrayed because of this, but I am not one. Following Vietnam I never searched for others' approval as to whether what we did was right or wrong. I personally have always been satisfied with my performance and that of the majority of fellow vets while we were there. The winning or losing of the war does not diminish my feelings in the slightest. Not only did I not need a parade or dinner as a sign of gratitude for my participation in the war, I sincerely didn't want one. After all, I'm the one who would have had to march in the parade (I hate to march—flat feet), and most testimonials are only slightly more exciting than watching butter melt. I had only one goal upon my return home and that was to see my family and friends.

Later, as a student at Kent State University, I may have on occasion been treated with some disrespect, but at other times I was treated very well. The most memorable occurrence was in late fall 1970 (following the shootings). The Kent State University Veterans Association (I was vice president) sponsored a weekend party for disabled vets from the Cleveland hospital. Many of those vets were paraplegics or quadraplegics. With the help of a local sorority we took them out for dinner, to a Kent State basketball game, and to the sorority house for a party.

Since the vets were in wheelchairs, we arranged for basketball seating on the floor behind one basket. Prior to the game the announcer told the crowd of the presence of our group over the P.A. system. Instantaneously the entire audience rose to their feet and gave a standing ovation that easily lasted for five minutes. At Kent State (the alleged hotbed of radicalism), I experienced my parade in a manner I'll never forget.

I have since been able to complete my master's degree on the GI Bill, have a terrific wife and son, a good middle-management job with a large corporation, and am successfully going about my life as the majority of Vietnam and prior war vets have done.

*"We Wanted a Soldier
at Our Table"*

*We should remember that, even during those troubled days
of the late Sixties and early Seventies when the soldiers were
coming home from Vietnam, there were American civilians
who welcomed them with the warmth that returning soldiers
have traditionally been offered. The parades may not have
been there for the soldiers, but individual Americans were—
individual Americans who wanted to say "thank you."*

*The letters in this section are from veterans who encoun-
tered those particular Americans, and who want us to know
about the random kindnesses and expressions of gratitude.*

*Interestingly, of the letters I received, numerically this
group was by far the smallest.*

GLENN ENDRESS, VAN NUYS, CALIFORNIA

I'm now forty years old. I turned twenty-one in Vietnam.
1968 was my "lost year." I spent New Year's Eve 1967 at
the Oakland Army Terminal waiting to ship over on Janu-

ary 1, and returned home Christmas Day 1968, arriving at
Fort Lewis, Washington.

After a very fast debriefing (after all, it was Christmas
Day), we were released to go and find the airport (yes, my
story did take place in an airport). I had a one-month leave
before reporting to Fort Hancock, New Jersey, to complete
the six months remaining of my two-year tour of duty.

I returned a sergeant/E5, having served with the 23rd Infantry Division (Americal) as a combat M.P. I spent most
of my time running convoys up and down Highway 1 on a
gun Jeep, resupplying artillery bases and other forward out-
posts with replacements and supplies. Every morning we
hoped the Marine mine sweep teams had done their jobs
properly. They usually did. Returning to the base camp in
the evening was a race against darkness ("Charlie owns the
night"), but we usually won the race. We used to call it "40
miles of bad road," after the old Duane Eddy tune. This is
just a little background so you'll know I wasn't a cook at the
officer's mess in Saigon. Now on to my experience at the
Seattle airport, which is as vivid to me now, 20 years later,
as any of my experiences in Vietnam.

During the Tet Offensive, I had occasion to pick up a MAS
36 French carbine, a VC weapon left over from the French
occupation. I kept it to bring home as a "war trophy." I still
have it. Army regulations prohibited sending it home by mail
or in hold-baggage, so you had to hand-carry it if you wanted
it (minus the bolt, of course, which could be sent in hold-
baggage). So I lugged it home along with my duffel bag.

Standing in line to purchase my ticket to L.A. at the airport was a heady experience to say the least. It was Christmas
Day, a beautiful day; the first "round-eyed" women I had
seen in a year were everywhere. There were two young girls,
probably college coeds, behind me in line to buy tickets also.
I'm holding the MAS 36, wearing my greens with all my
acquired "fruit salad" and other assorted bullshit, feeling

like Audie Murphy. I turned and smiled at the girls just knowing they would be swept off their feet by me, the returning hero.

No, they didn't spit on me, not in the physical sense. Instead, they gave me the dirtiest looks I've received before or since. They stared at me the way one would stare at an admitted child molester who feels no remorse and has vowed to molest again.

They said nothing. I said "Merry Christmas!" They said nothing. I quickly turned and faced front. It took a few minutes before my turn came to buy my ticket; it seemed like an hour. During those few minutes I listened to a diatribe which was not directed specifically at me, but at the "war-mongering, village-burning, woman-raping, baby-killing scum" called soldiers—American soldiers.

It was a rather loud conversation that began something like this:

Girl No. 1: "I wonder how many children they killed with rifles like that?"

Girl No. 2: "I don't know, but you'd have to be really proud of what you did to carry it around in an airport."

I bought my ticket and retreated to the observation deck for a three-hour wait. I hadn't realized how the opinion of a great many American people about the war had swung so drastically between June '67 when I was drafted, to almost January 1969.

Alone with my thoughts on the observation deck looking out at the gorgeous snow-capped mountains on that day of blue, blue skies and billowy white clouds, I tried to put those two girls out of my mind and concentrate on what was to come: Mom, Dad, and Linda, my fiancée, waiting for me at LAX, just a few hours away.

Suddenly a voice behind me said, "Merry Christmas, Sarge." I turned thinking it was another G.I., probably someone I had arrived at Fort Lewis with. Instead, there stood a middle-aged civilian man and his skinny kid of about thirteen with long, straight, blond hair to his shoulders.

The man asked me what time my flight was leaving. Suspicious after what had happened in the ticket line, I asked why. He said he'd like me to come to his home for Christmas dinner if I had the time and wasn't able to be home.

I thanked him and said no, I didn't want to take the chance of missing my flight. I told him I knew there were some guys in the terminal who weren't flying out until late that night, and maybe one of them would like to take him up on his offer.

He said all right and wished me Merry Christmas again and started to walk away with the kid. They took a few steps and I called to him and asked why he would ask a perfect stranger to come to his house for Christmas dinner. He said his son had died in Vietnam that past year, and "we wanted a soldier at our table for Christmas dinner."

Then they turned and left. I turned and looked back at the snow-capped mountains and began to cry.

JAMES GRITZ, SANDY VALLEY, NEVADA

I have also heard these "spitting rumors" since 1965, and I have had just the opposite experience.

True enough, I was a Green Beret with sixth-degree karate black belt; I have 60-plus decorations for heroism and achievement. At five feet ten inches and 210 pounds, I probably looked like a tank destroyer to the druggies and undernourished hippies of the '60s and early '70s. No one person or group would have dared spit at me then—or now.

But quite to the contrary, in those days I couldn't pay for my own drink in a bar. I never bought a meal in San Francisco (center of discontent)! Both coming and going to Vietnam out of Travis Air Force Base, each time (over a period of four years) I entered and exited through the city using San

Francisco hotels, restaurants, and public facilities. No one ever walked up and said, "Let me buy you that meal, soldier." Instead it was more subtle—on no less than six occasions the cashier simply said, "It has been taken care of." I even pressed to identify my benefactor. Each time it was the same—"just anonymous."

Once, having left San Francisco by car, my brother (a U.S. Navy Vietnam vet) and I were driving to our home in Tucson, Arizona—at 100 miles per hour. About dawn an Arizona highway patrolman caught up to me. As I got out of the car (still in uniform), he asked, "Are you just home from Nam?" I replied, "Yes, sir." He waved me on with a gentle reprimand to "please drive more sanely to arrive alive."

Another year (my Vietnam service was from 1964 through November 1968), I took my family to Las Vegas to see the stage show "Hello Dolly." Upon entering the casino I noticed an around-the-corner line behind the "Reservations" chain. An usher laughed and told me the show had been "sold out for a month." As my mom, dad, a friend, and I started to depart disappointed, a manager seeing us asked, "Are you home from Vietnam?" Upon my affirmative reply, he escorted us to the first row of tables, with dinner and the show "on the house."

During those years (1964–1968) I ranged from California, Oklahoma, Arizona, Virginia, Washington, D.C., without a single incident of discourtesy. I have only cited highlights of the outstanding treatment I received. Friends and family always hosted parties and block-support gatherings. After Vietnam I served two years at the Language Institute, Monterey, California; another year at the University of Nebraska; two years at the Pentagon—all of this without incident. I attended the American University as a grad student for another two years without a single insult. As a student, I found younger people who opposed the war most interested in hearing my opinion of why we were in Vietnam. I am not a brawler, and gave no intimidation other than an ordinarily "not very handsome" appearance.

Personally, I'm very proud and pleased with America and the way Americans have treated me and the fellow vets I know—both during the war and now. I'm even more encouraged by the way Americans have come out strong and unrelenting for our POWs and MIAs. I believe the American people are beautiful. We are certainly a nation blessed. I have never and don't believe Americans in general would spit on anybody for any reason.

The enemies I've fought have been overseas. My countrymen have always made me glad to be back home.

BOB BOUGHTON, FREDERICKTOWN, OHIO

I have a true story that involves a "hippie."

I was recovering from injuries received in Vietnam at a military hospital near Philadelphia. While waiting for a bus home there, an elderly woman came up to me, looked me square in the face, and called me a hired killer.

But as I said, my story included a "hippie." A young lady dressed in bell-bottoms, love beads, and a peace symbol came up to me as the elderly woman walked away. She looked me in the face and told me she was sorry for the way the returning vets were being treated.

I never got the chance to thank her, nor even got her name. But I could never forget her face and those few kind words.

CARL LINDBECK, DE PERE, WISCONSIN

Please bear with me as I recount my tale. I returned from Vietnam in October 1969 with a buddy named Eddie who was from Chicago. When we finally were released from the holding base to make the return to our hometowns we waited in the airport for our plane.

We were of course dressed in full military uniform and I was carrying a Russian rifle which I had picked up as a war souvenir. We stopped in an airport bar for a drink and an older couple approached us. They offered to buy us a drink to show their appreciation for what we had just gone through. They spoke to us for a short time, and while I don't recall the details of the conversation, I do remember the warmth of their voices and the smiles they treated us to.

Eddie and I were somewhat amused because we had literally been out of contact with the ''world'' for more than a year. The remainder of our trip was uneventful and except for our families I don't think anyone else noticed that we had returned. Most of the people I knew simply ignored the fact and never spoke about it.

DOUGLAS A. BRUCE, COLORADO SPRINGS, COLORADO

I have talked to many disabled vets during my work at the Disabled Veterans Corporate Center here in Colorado Springs. I haven't found one disabled vet who admitted that he was spat upon, whether in an airport or not, hippies or not. I would like to relay one of my many trips back to the U.S. of A. during the conflict. I served from May 1965 through June 1971.

During my service in Vietnam I took the opportunity to extend my service tour in exchange for a free 30-day leave to any free port to which U.S. flagships flew. On a trip down to Florida, I was flying from California to Montgomery, Alabama to visit the wife and children of one of my friends who was in Vietnam. I had Christmas packages for the children that wouldn't have arrived in time for Christmas—that was the biggest reason for the visit.

Talk about a surprise. I tried to rent a car. I got a car, all right—but no charge. I drove to my friend's address to find that it was his wife's bowling night. I went to the bowling alley—talk about a commotion when I walked in wearing my green Army uniform with the few ribbons I had acquired. I had more offers of beer, sandwiches, Cokes, etc. The league my friend's wife was bowling in was already in the last game and they were going to some steak house. We went, had steak dinners—I couldn't pay for mine. The proprietor wouldn't take my money.

It was like this my entire stay of three days, including free hotel rooms. It was really unbelievable. Also, of the 16 visits back to the U.S. during my service, on six of those visits I was placed in first class on the airplane and not charged.

DAVID VOLK, PIERRE, SOUTH DAKOTA

Bad treatment does not have to take as vulgar a form as spitting. In many cases it was nothing more than a cold look of contempt when you walked through an airport or the constant haranguing by people who wanted to debate or argue the war when they caught you in a public place. Maybe the worst was a feeling that they just wanted you to go away; that you were nothing more than a bad reminder of a bad war.

I remember being in a Seattle airport bar one time, standing off by myself to avoid other people, when a middle-aged man came up and asked me if I was a Vietnam vet. Reluctantly, I admitted it, expecting the usual debate to begin. Instead, this gentleman turned to the bartender and in the best tradition of World War II said, "Get the soldier a beer." It was the nicest thing that anyone did for me during the final year that I wore my uniform.

If the number of "spitting" incidents are inflated, it doesn't change for a minute the feelings of rejection and scorn that a bunch of depressed and confused young men experienced when they returned home from doing what their country told them to do.

JOHN MCCAMLEY, COPPERAS COVE, TEXAS

I did three tours in Vietnam as an infantryman, and I never saw any of the "incidents" that were supposed to be happening all the time at airports. None of my friends saw the incidents. Some mention should be made of the so-called silent majority who supported the GI in Vietnam. Many were very active in that support.

I was the platoon leader of an understrength infantry platoon that was "adopted" by a local of the Steel Workers Union of America back home. They were fantastic people. I mentioned in one letter to them about one of the men busting his one and only pipe during a firefight. A couple weeks later we received a large carton airmailed first class. You guessed it—pipes, tobacco, pipe cleaners, etc.

When I finished my tour in May 1967 I decided to stop off and thank that union on behalf of the men. I wrote to the union and told them I was coming, but I failed to give them a flight number. I arrived at 1 a.m., and much to my surprise there were four officials from the Steel Workers local union waiting for me, including the president. I was put up in one of the better hotels and was given a grand tour of the city. That was my welcome back to the U.S.A., and I'll never forget it.

Too many would-be veterans from Vietnam are using Vietnam as a reason why they are messed up. But I'd better get off my soapbox.

MRS. JIMMY LAMBERT, ABILENE, TEXAS

During my husband's Air Force career, I waited at lots of airport gates for him to return. In September 1966, when he returned from Vietnam, I was at the gate to meet his plane at Love Field in Dallas. He was treated with respect. If anything was said by people, it was, "Glad to see you made it home."

ROBERT C. HUNT, LAKEWOOD, COLORADO

Just one week ago, my wife introduced me to an ex-Marine, who was in Vietnam the same time I was. During our brief conversation, this Marine aviator recalled his Vietnam experience with many references to drugs, the black market, and flying combat missions stoned. He mentioned being spat upon when he returned to the Oakland, California processing center in December 1970. His comment on the incident was that he was "more stoned than the spitters, so why were they spitting?" The man's story was believable, but quite the opposite of my own experience.

I returned to the States in mid-April 1971, through Fort Lewis, Washington and perhaps the geographical location is significant. I was quite tan, in terrific physical shape, had a chestful of decorations, and was quite obviously returning from duty in Vietnam. I had a five-hour wait for a late-night flight to Minneapolis. I spent much of my time in the airport's restaurant, having a leisurely dinner with another returning veteran. The bill for two of us—we were very hungry—was $37. It was stamped "Paid." The waitress explained that an older gentleman sitting next to us had paid our bill when he left, and had told her to say thanks to us.

I arrived in Minneapolis around 4 o'clock in the morning. I was three weeks early and was surprising my family, so I had called friends to pick me up. While waiting for my friends, I was offered a ride home by four individuals, including one man arriving home from vacation with his wife and two children. He lived in the opposite direction and had been up all night, but was willing to drive because he and his wife did not want me to have to wait for a taxi to complete my journey home.

My thanks go out to the people at both airports, total strangers, who by their warmth and gratitude made my return from Vietnam a welcome one, and one that I will always remember fondly.

DENNIS E. COURNOYER, LAS VEGAS, NEVADA

Several things come to mind very clearly. In May of 1967 I went to Vietnam with hundreds of other guys just like me. Boys and men of all shapes, sizes, and colors. Some of us stayed together over there; some didn't. What can be said from my standpoint is we were there because we were needed. My view is that of a healthy, complete, forty-year-old man, and I speak only for myself.

In May 1968 many of us returned to the States wondering what we had done. Upon arrival at the airport in Seattle, the Army provided new uniforms. The next thing most of us wanted to do was to contact our families to let them know we were back in the "real world."

Having taken care of our personal attentions we focused on the nearest refreshment stand. Some wanted "real" beer, some whiskey, and still others Coke, Pepsi, Dr Pepper, coffee or tea.

The group with the inclination for the hard stuff went to the bar. We were loud, happy, and filled with many other emotions, but I will never forget what happened over the next several minutes. A man in the lounge with a 10-gallon hat and a million-dollar heart, whose name I never knew, welcomed us back to America and thanked us for what we had done. He then put 10 hundred-dollar bills on the bar, announced that our money was not any good, and started applauding.

The other patrons joined in, and then we knew what we experienced was appreciated not only by that group but by tens of millions of other Americans. Those few minutes at the airport watering hole made me realize I was welcome in my country.

S. DUKE, DENVER, COLORADO

Bear with me here, I'm not a writer, but I'll give her a go. I left Vietnam on March 20, 1971, for Okinawa, hit El Toro on the 24th. Several of us got together and took a cab from there to Los Angeles International Airport. What a ride—the first thing I'd been in that went over 35 miles per hour in a year.

The airport in Los Angeles was bustling as usual. There were lots of military types roaming around—from all of the services. Probably a real common sight there—in fact there were so many military men that no one seemed to pay attention to any of us. I didn't expect a parade, but I was twenty years old and puffed up due to my chest full of new ribbons and happiness at being back in the "world." It sure would be nice if someone noticed me—so I remember thinking.

Another sergeant and I went into one of the bars after checking in at our airlines and dumping our seabags. Bryce had about six hours before his flight and I had four. Sgt. Bryce ordered the drinks because he was over 21 and the bartender never asked me for ID. Then I thought I was getting away with something, but now I figure the bartender wasn't a dummy. He knew I wasn't 21.

The bartender didn't take any of our money for the drinks. After about the third drink we asked him about it. He said that our money was no good. A guy at the bar was buying all we wanted. As it turned out the "guy" at the bar was Jim Davis (you know—Jock from "Dallas," the TV show, before he died). Anyway, he came over to us and said anybody who served their country didn't buy drinks when he was around. After four hours of that, they about had to pour me onto my plane.

There were lots of "hippies" (if there ever was such a thing) at the airport in L.A. and in Denver when I landed at Stapleton. For the most part they didn't pay any attention to me and I ignored them. I too had heard the stories of guys getting spit on and wanted none. I waited at the airport about 45 minutes for my sister to come pick me up—boring since no one noticed me.

My sister and I arrived at my parents' house—it was a typical Saturday night. Except for Mom. She got to me before I cleared the front porch, a hug that squeezed so hard I thought she would do what the North Vietnamese couldn't. Boy—do I remember that. No big deal was made of my return by my family. After all, my brother-in-law had been in Vietnam in 1965–66 and as I got home my brother was still in Vietnam. But that was some hug.

I had gone in the service when I was seventeen years old. Got out at the age of twenty. I flew a lot between August 1968 and August of 1971. I probably showed the "hippies" more hostility than they aimed at me. Seventeen wasn't a good year for understanding. I was an eighteen-year-old corporal when I got stranded in San Francisco by a military flight. I was trying to get to the bus station, on foot, when the guy who passed for the hippie stereotype image picked me up.

He drove me as far as I needed to go. Said he had a brother in Vietnam.

BERT G. LANDAU, TUCSON, ARIZONA

I had two tours of duty in Vietnam . . . the first from early September 1967 to late September 1968, and the second from February 1970 to December 1970. Both tours were in combat units. For the first tour, I served with an Infantry Company and then an Artillery Battery. Most of the second tour was with an Artillery Battery.

Nobody spit on me either time I came home. But they were very different experiences.

First the good one. I landed back in America at some Air Force base outside of Seattle, Washington. Those of us that were not getting out of the military were allowed to "process" through the receiving station quickly and get to the nearest airport. A group of us took a cab to the Seattle airport and tried to get a seat on a plane.

It was indescribably exciting being back in the U.S. Everything was green, peaceful, and beautiful. I still remember that cab ride vividly. We rode silently, locked in our own thoughts as the cab sped down a highway to the airport. There was no more danger. At last, I was home. But I was more exhausted than I could ever remember in my life. The day before the "freedom bird" took off from Vietnam, I left my unit and flew to Cahm Rahn Bay. We had been digging in new defensive positions for three days when I left my unit. That's a 24-hour-a-day job. After what seemed like just a few hours in Cahm Rahn Bay, I was going home! I couldn't sleep on the airplane—that 18 hours on the airplane seemed like months.

By the time the cab stopped at the Seattle airport, I was practically dead on my feet. There was no harassment there. In fact, some lady came up to me after I had purchased a ticket and asked if I felt all right. I didn't and told her so. She said there was a lounge for servicemen in another part of the airport where I could lie down until my plane arrived. Since I had a four-hour wait for the plane, that sounded too good to be true. I followed her to the lounge.

Another lady in the lounge said that, since I had four hours to wait, there were beds available for me to use. She offered to have someone watch over my bags and took me to the beds. She said she would have someone wake me in time for my flight. There was a man in the room to watch over the sleeping men and make certain they were awakened in time as well as to make sure nothing was stolen. He woke me up a little early and said there was a shower available if I wanted to use it before my flight. He found a towel and some soap. I headed for the shower. Afterward, he had someone carry my bags to the airline departure area. I was still a little "rocky."

Those folks in Seattle, all volunteers, were great and I've always wanted to thank them but didn't know how. They really made me feel "home" again.

The other trip home from Vietnam took me to Los Angeles. If the airport in Seattle was at one end of a "good-bad" scale, L.A. was at the other end.

When I walked into the terminal, carrying my bags, a group of six or seven kids about my own age headed over to me as I staggered along with the baggage. Other servicemen were also in the terminal and they all seemed to be with a group of these kids. Now, I'm not a big person. And after a year out in the field, we all looked emaciated. I think I weighed about 135 pounds then, all five feet eight of me. And I'm not very intimidating looking either. In fact, the other guys I served with in the field always used to remark that I didn't look like I belonged out in the boonies—even though I had been there through some of the hardest fighting of the entire war.

The conversation in the airport went something like this:

The largest guy in the group walked up to me and said, "Just back from Nam?" I said yes, avoiding his eyes, and continuing to move toward the area where I would board my next flight to Tucson. "Whatja do over there?" he asked. By this time the other kids had surrounded me and I couldn't move without having one of them move out of my way. "Just my job," I replied, and then said "Excuse me" as I started to move past them. None of them moved so I was stuck in the middle of their group.

I can't call these kids hippies. They looked just like we

did before we went to Vietnam. They were a typical slice of young Americana—the young man or young woman next door. Sure, some of them wore their hair longer than I used to do, but they looked just like the people I had gone to college with two years before then. Two or three of them were girls—good-looking girls—the kind I used to date. They were the kind of kids I thought I still was. But to them, I was NOT one of them. I had been to Vietnam. I was different. I didn't want to be different, but the choice wasn't mine. I will never forget the hatred on their faces as they confronted me. I will never understand how that hatred can exist for one of their own kind, someone they don't even know.

One of the other boys in the group said, "Man, you don't belong here anymore. People like you are supposed to stay in Nam and die—just like you did to the Vietnamese." I replied, "How do you know what I did?" One of the girls said to me, "We already know what you did. You don't belong here—there's no place for you in America anymore. Just go away and die. And I hope you die as miserably as the Vietnamese you killed."

I said, "Excuse me," and tried to continue moving. This time, I bumped into the guy blocking my path. The very pretty girl standing next to him didn't look as good after she said, "That fucker bumped John. You can't get away with that here, asshole—we're not Vietnamese." And then she pushed me and John pushed me, too. He said, "We don't take that kind of shit from baby killers, you bastard." I replied, "Sorry, but I have to get my flight. I didn't kill any babies and you got the wrong guy. Go pick on someone else."

These people were what I thought were my peers and the things they said made me feel ashamed to be there, in uniform. I just wanted to disappear.

The confrontation got worse. One of the girls grabbed for my duffel bag, exclaiming, "We're not through with you yet." I yanked the duffel bag away from her. It contained the first pictures of my only son, who had been born while I was in Vietnam. The girl fell down. One of the guys hit me in the face.

I staggered backwards from the blow, falling outside their little circle. Suddenly, I wasn't so overcome by shame anymore. I was angry. The same kind of anger you get in Nam when you are ambushed or under attack. I wanted to hit back. I dropped my bags and faced the small group. I knew that, if they wanted to fight, I would do my damndest to make sure I was the only one who walked away. "Okay," I said, "you want to play. Now, I want to play, too. Which one of you motherfuckers wants to play first?" I reached for the big guy, the one that accosted me first, but he shrank away from me. The others backed away with him.

Well, they got out of there quickly, exclaiming loudly that they had found another "crazy killer"—and maybe I was for a few minutes there. No one spit at me that day in the L.A. airport, but it still felt the same. I walked on to my terminal, feeling a lot differently about being back home again. Walking through the terminal, I guess the expression on my face was different than when I entered. Very suddenly, it felt like there was no home to come back to.

BEN LIMBAUGH, BATAVIA, ILLINOIS

When I was flying home, trying to mentally prepare for what might await me at the airport, I realized that I wanted neither praise nor scorn when I got back. And I got neither when I arrived back. On my plane to O'Hare I sat next to a good-looking nurse who told me "thanks" and that she was glad I got home alive.

Later, on campus at Illinois State University in Normal, Illinois, a street mime protesting the war jumped in front of a friend of mine and me, shouting "Do you know that people

are fighting and dying in Vietnam right now?'' I replied,
"Yeah, I just got back.'' The girl burst into tears, and apol-
ogized to me.

BOB LEITH, SAN JOSE, CALIFORNIA

My story has a little different twist, and I still get goose-
bumps when I tell it.

I left for Vietnam on August 24, 1968, and I flew Hueys
around Tay Nihn and Cambodia until August 17, 1969. When
I returned to the base that day, my operations sergeant came
running out and told me I was going home one week early.

Within 30 hours, I was at Travis Air Force Base, and called
my in-laws-to-be in San Jose and announced my early arrival
and asked where my fiancée was. They replied that she was
on her last flight as a stewardess with American Airlines, and
was due to land at the San Francisco airport in about three
hours.

I immediately got on a bus and made it to the gate as her
plane taxied in. The door opened, and here I am standing,
looking at her in the plane. She flew the New York-San Francisco route pretty regularly, so had told the passengers that
this was her last flight, because I was due home from Vietnam in another week, and we were to be married on September 6.

So, needless to say, you can imagine the emotions. We
are in each other's arms, and as the people come off the plane
there are cheers, pats on the back, and all kinds of congrat-
ulations.

After our wedding, we flew across the U.S., stopping in
El Paso, Dallas, Washington, D.C., and New York, and I
never had a bad experience. I went back for a second tour in
1971–1972, and still did not.

MARCY MAUGHAN, NAPERVILLE, ILLINOIS

My husband, Phil Maughan, spent a year in Vietnam in 1970–1971. When he returned we were living in Dayton, Ohio. My daughter and I, along with Phil's parents and brother and sister, went to the airport to meet his plane. At that time, one had to disembark from the plane and walk to the terminal.

The family arrived at the airport, happy and eager. My father-in-law struck up a conversation with the airline employee at the gate, inside the terminal where we were waiting. When the employee discovered why we were waiting, he was able to get special permission for my daughter and me to stand outside, at the base of the steps of the plane, and wait for my husband at that point. That way, we would be the first thing he would see when he got off the plane.

I have always been very grateful for that act of kindness the airline employee showed. At no time was my husband treated with anything but kindness while at the airport or on the trip home.

TIM CHELLING, SAN DIEGO, CALIFORNIA

I served in the U.S. Air Force from 1970–1974. During that period I received two free trips to Southeast Asia. The first trip was a deployment of our wing to Thailand and Vietnam.

I returned to our home base in South Carolina with other members of our unit after seven months. We stepped off the plane to be greeted by a crowd of cheering relatives and friends from the base. I was personally met by the members of my unit who had already returned or who had stayed behind in Myrtle Beach. They toasted me with champagne on the ramp around midnight to welcome me back.

My return from my second assignment in Southeast Asia

coincided with the end of my enlistment. As I waited in the San Francisco airport for my final flight in uniform to my home of record in San Diego, a little girl approached me. She appeared to be seven or eight years old. She first asked me if I worked for the airlines. After I explained that I was in the Air Force, she then simply asked me if I had been away a long time. I said yes. All she did then was say: "You have a really nice smile," and turned away. It was the nicest welcome I could have arranged.

Those are my memories of my homecomings. No parades, no billboards, it was still lonely, but I ran into some good human beings.

PETER MOYLAN, SAN FRANCISCO, CALIFORNIA

I served in the United States Marine Corps from 1965 to 1969. The last year and a half I was stationed in New York City at the Marine Corps recruiting station. My friends are all amazed when I tell them of what the uniform meant in New York City. Here are some examples of what happened to me:

In full dress blues, I walked into a Broadway theatre with my date. The usher collecting tickets at the door grabbed my hand, vigorously shaking it and thanking me for what I was doing.

In a fancy midtown restaurant (at the time one of the best in New York), I was treated in an absolutely professional manner, with grace and aplomb, despite the fact that I was in uniform and I'm sure that the waiter had to think I couldn't leave much of a tip.

At another restaurant, I had lunch with a young woman. The bill, in 1969, was $40. When I asked for the check, the waiter, with a great deal of respect in his voice, told me that it had been taken care of.

I always urged my fellow Marines to go out on the town

in uniform, because it invariably led to free drinks from former servicemen as well as making it easier to meet girls (which was important to me, because I was never very macho or good at that).

When a Marine photographer dropped a full bottle of acid used in the developing process, shattering the bottle and forcing us to evacuate the building, a group of us went to a nearby fire station. The firemen allowed us—actually welcomed us—to ride the fire trucks down Seventh Avenue back to our office. (We had only gone there to borrow gas masks to clean up the mess.)

On St. Patrick's Day in 1969, I walked into a bar on the Upper East Side at the end of the parade route, announced that "I am Sergeant Moylan, I'm as Irish as can be, and if you'll buy me a drink I'll prove it to you." I never spent a dime that day and I'm sure it was the uniform.

I stood in line at a theater to buy tickets for "Hair" on my lunchbreak, in full uniform, and it was as if I just blended into the group. There was no reaction, one way or the other.

At no time was I ever personally the recipient of negative comments, much less being spat upon. Further, when I went home (off-duty), I used to hang out at a local college establishment called Bill's Meadowbrook, nestled amidst the campus of Hofstra University in Hempstead, Long Island (where the New York Jets hold training camp). Most of the people I associated with were college students (some of whom I had gone to high school with). All knew I was in the Marines. Despite prevalent anti-war attitudes, I never faced a negative moment there. In fact, one of my fondest moments occurred when the Marines' district office in Garden City, Long Island, threw a party for wounded sailors and Marines recuperating at St. Alban's Naval Hospital in Queens. An officer knew that I had grown up nearby and thought that I might know some girls who would like to come to the party. I happened to know a couple of girls from a sorority at Hofstra, from the local telephone company, and a couple who were nurses. Among them, they managed to bring more girls to the party than there were sailors and Marines! I was something of a hero to the guys after that one!

BRUCE WERNER, SAN FRANCISCO, CALIFORNIA

I spent two-and-a-half years in Vietnam (Air Force) and traveled cross-country in the U.S. maybe a dozen times, always in uniform, between January 1968 and June 1970.

My experiences were so universally the opposite of the people who say they were spat upon that I have to write.

Never was anyone, of any political stripe, age, or sex, anything but nice, to say the least. Some of my friends thought I was a little nuts to drop out of college, give up my deferment, and enlist. I even VOLUNTEERED for Nam, then voluntarily extended the tours.

My experience during those times include:

A man who gave me his airline ticket so I could get home for Christmas when all the flights were full;

A young woman with long hair in Seattle who gave me a flower and a hug and told me it wasn't me, but the government;

And every airline desk agent and flight crew that always seemed to make sure I got on my "standby" flight and always wished me "good luck."

Many Americans may have hated their war but they sure loved their GIs. Maybe this is my little way of saying "Thanks" almost 20 years later.

Arlen B. Coyle, Richmond, Virginia

Right away you should know that I wasn't spat upon when I came back.

I returned from Vietnam consistent with typical military timetables: in the middle of the night. The plane landed at Travis Air Force Base in Oakland, California, at some beastly pre-dawn hour on March 31, 1968, but no one complained of the scheduling. I was a young Navy lieutenant with a good suntan, money in my pocket, and orders to the Navy's newest aircraft carrier, the USS John F. Kennedy, which was still under construction in Virginia. Before reporting to my new command, however, I had a month's leave due me and I was on my way to Natchez, Mississippi, my childhood home.

Two things remain foremost in my memory of arriving at Travis AFB: my kissing the ground when I stepped off the boarding ramp, and the rows of aluminum coffins containing the other young Americans who returned in our plane's cargo hold. No more kisses for them. It was an emotional seesaw, with elation and joy on one end and survivor's guilt on the other. Being spared has a price, too.

I called the first air carrier in the Yellow Pages—American Airlines—to reserve a seat on the next available flight to New Orleans. American had a redeye leaving at some ridiculous hour, but could only put me on standby, provided I could get to San Francisco International Airport in short order.

Luck was truly with me that night. I hailed the first available taxi and inquired of the driver whether he could get me to the airport in time to ''make my bird.'' He assured me he could. He did. It was the wildest taxi ride I have ever had in the States, and included the driver's non-stop narrative of the sights along the way, his ideas for winning the war, and his women-problems.

I was ready to tip big when we arrived at the airport, but he refused payment—he said it was his cab and he could charge whatever he damn-well pleased. I insisted on paying him but he insisted on refusing. I had a knife from Vietnam in one of my bags, and we finally agreed that he would take the knife in lieu of payment.

Things went smoothly at the airport—perhaps it was too early for the peace freaks and others who made things difficult for people in military uniform. The people at the American Airlines ticket counter could not have been more courteous and helpful. They put me aboard the plane as standby, which resulted in my being the last person to board. Of course, I wasn't complaining, even though it meant I was seated all the way aft, across from the plane's galley.

Shortly after we were airborne it began to sink in that I was actually going home. To a Southerner, going home is always an emotion-filled event. This trip was especially so.

The stewardesses were initially busy tending to all the people and doing all the things they do at the first of a flight, but things soon settled down. Two of them retired aft to the galley and struck up a conversation with me. The usual small talk ensued—"Where are you coming from? How long have you been gone? What was it like? Where are you going?" A few jokes, a few "sea stories." One animated topic led to another as we crossed the continent.

Then one of them asked me The Question.

I've heard that people struck by lightning often sense the strike moments before it actually arrives—they describe it as a tingling of the skin presaging the bolt.

That was the sensation I experienced when she asked me:

"Do you have a place to stay in New Orleans?"

You know how a pinball machine jerks into life when you drop your coin into the slot, and lights flash and bells ring and the balls clatter into the chute awaiting the start of the game? Same thing, only different; I knew it wasn't intended as a simple "yes" or "no" question.

For me, a new game had begun. The stewardess who asked The Question and I had three of the best days of my young life there in New Orleans. I seem to recall that we went out to eat once, but I couldn't swear to it—the rest of the time we stayed at her place.

I assure you, I wasn't spat upon. Those three days and nights were better than any parade.

"Some Things Are Worse Than Being Spat On"

Many veterans thought that the spitting question missed the point entirely. What did it matter if someone literally spat on them? The manner in which America generally treated the soldiers who were coming home, they said, was far more telling than whether or not, by happenstance, an individual veteran encountered a person who was unkind enough to spit.

In explaining this, the veterans provided insights into yet another corner of this whole perplexing story. They, too, had heard the spitting tales for years—and they knew that, in the end, the ramifications of the Vietnam homecoming experience went far beyond the confines of whether a particular man felt a stranger's spit hit him.

J. C. PENNINGTON, CHANNELVIEW, TEXAS

I returned to the United States on August 4, 1969, after having served a year as a helicopter pilot for the U.S. Army in Vietnam.

Nothing happened immediately after my return home, and I was stationed at Fort Rucker, Alabama, the U.S. Army Aviation Center. In October I flew to Chicago to meet the widow of one of my flight school classmates who had been killed in Vietnam just prior to his scheduled return home. Flying from Alabama to Chicago, the airline lost my luggage and all I had was the uniform I was traveling in.

I was staying at the Drake Hotel in Chicago, and about midnight I decided to go out for something to eat. Since my Army dress-green uniform was all I had, that's what I was wearing as I walked down Walton Street toward Rush to find a restaurant.

As you know, Friday night on Rush Street can be tumultuous at any time, but to a Vietnam vet wearing a uniform in 1969, it was a most unpleasant place. As I stood on the corner of Walton and Rush waiting for a traffic light to change, one car full of "hippies," slowed down, and two of the passengers leaned out of the window and started screaming—murderer, baby killer, and other similar pleasantries. I had walked less than a block on Rush Street when three people approaching me on the sidewalk asked if any of my ribbons were awarded for killing women and children.

Regardless of my military background and training, I did not, and do not, like physical violence. However, at that point I didn't much care. I stopped in front of the three and started walking toward them with the intent of swinging at the first one I reached. I did not particularly care what happened to me at that point. In the preceding year I had faced people a lot tougher than these clowns, and these guys weren't shooting at me with anything but their mouths.

True to their colors, all three turned and ran away from me. At that point I had lost my appetite and decided to go back to the hotel and try to go to sleep.

The schizophrenic nature of the time confronted me as I was waiting in the Drake's lobby for an elevator. An older couple, gently and happily inebriated, were waiting with me to go to their room. As we got on the elevator the happy, grandmotherly half of the pair eyed my uniform with ribbons, aviator wings, and quietly said, "You look so handsome in that uniform. It makes me so proud every time I see one of you boys in it." Thanks to that short elevator ride I was able to get some sleep that night.

Did I get spit on? No, I did not. I wish I had. It would have been easier than listening to what I had to hear that night on Rush Street.

MARVIN D. McCREARY, ADDISON, ILLINOIS

I guess it really is up to how one interprets being "spat upon." When 15 other vets and myself landed at Travis Air Force Base in California, we were met by a mob of angry teenagers who actually threw eggs and tomatoes as well as a few other vegetables at us while they were screaming that we were baby killers and murderers.

And why would we let something like this go by at the moment, uncontested? It is very simple. We had just spent a year of our lives fighting for what we believed our country wanted even though we had been terrified. We were exhausted, drained, listless. We just wanted the peace and quiet that we believed we would have at home in our land. Ruthless and seemingly cold-hearted things happened over there where we had served our country, but that is war, and it has happened in every war.

Think about us veterans who are now dying of various conditions from the dioxin poisoning due to exposure to Agent Orange spraying by our government. Our own government is actually spitting on us because it will not do anything about helping to find a cure for us or care for us who have this service-related condition. If this is not being spat upon, I don't know what is.

Then there is the issue of the POW/MIAs. Our government is trying to dismiss the whole issue and just forget about these men. The government did not forget about the POWs in other wars, so why this one? Our government knows the POWs are there, but the government is spitting on them.

Maybe all these things are not actually spewing someone else's saliva on us vets, but as far as I am concerned, that is exactly what it is.

PRESTON STERN, PHILMONT, NEW YORK

I have a fairly unique perspective, because I was one of the few vets who worked both sides of the fence. I was an active war protester before, during, and after my tour of duty as a U.S. infantryman in Vietnam. Let me say up-front that though no spit ever fell on me, I find the stories of spat-upon vets entirely believable.

I allowed myself to be inducted (it was the Army's third try) in April, 1967. I made no bones about my opposition to the war and to the concept of "military solutions" to political problems. Everybody in the Army who knew of me knew of my beliefs. If you know how the Army works, you know that it was guaranteed that I would be assigned to be trained as a combat infantryman and scheduled to ship out to Nam that September.

All through training I was a marked man. I did my best to stand up for my principles while mastering the lessons of war making. The special treatment I received from drill sergeants, officers, and some of the GIs was pretty rough sometimes. But it was no worse than I got from some of my so-called friends while home on leave before shipping out.

I know what it is like to be called baby killer and to be scorned. No doubt many of the taunts were considered to be constructive. I remember one fellow asked me, "Haven't you ever heard the song 'Universal Soldier'?" and I replied, truthfully, "Man, I sing that song in the barracks just about everyday!"

The point here is that when emotions run high sympathy for the other fellow goes down. These folks back home knew me and knew my anti-war activities. But they were in no mood to listen, to learn if my experiences had any meaning for them. It was my ardent hope that they did and would, but some people couldn't hear that.

Do not forget what those days were really like. By 1968 the anti-war demonstrations were increasingly violent—remember the "Days of Rage"? Though it was typical for a GI, especially a Vietnam vet, to see all anti-war protesters as "hippies," the reality is that many had become hardened warriors of their own kind. They took on Chicago cops and the National Guard, so why not the occasional GI?

I am sure that not every GI who suffered abuse from a citizen was a returning combat vet. Many were clerks, or cooks, or medics, or something. No doubt many never even left the U.S. They were just men in uniform who got caught in an emotional crossfire. These men were not cartoons, they were humans with complex emotions and, though certainly hardened and tough, they were just as likely to be very fragile.

Incidentally, to finish my own story, I did go to Vietnam in September 1967, and served in the field with an outfit known as the 4th Battalion of the 9th Infantry, 25th Infantry Division. In November I quit the war. I decided the time had come to be true to myself and so I laid down my weapon and submitted to court martial rather than martial arts. After a stint in the stockade at Long Binh—we called it Camp LBJ, for Long Binh Jail—I was returned to the 4th of the 9th while waiting for a discharge to be processed. I got back to the world in May 1968. And sure as shooting, many of the same people who had been so eager to condemn me before were now eager to line up and tell me what a great thing I had done.

I brushed them away. Their praise did not interest me. I cared much more for the opinion of the grunts back in the 4th of the 9th. After I returned to the base from Camp LBJ—while I was waiting to go home, leaving them behind—they told me I was the smartest man in the Army.

These days I still speak out for peace. Like most of us, I long for an end to the arms race and hope mankind can grow up enough to stop killing each other. I pray that my sons will never have to go to war. But secretly, I am proud of having earned a Combat Infantryman's Badge, of having shared the experience of Vietnam.

BONITA WHARTON, SAN JOSE, CALIFORNIA

Like so many of the 2 million soldiers who went to Vietnam, my husband, George, was drafted. He did not want to go, but he did. He did not go with enthusiasm or gung-ho great patriotism. He went because of his unadorned, unembellished sense of duty.

He did not stay long in Vietnam. Thirty-three days into his tour as a medic and a month before his twenty-first birthday, he was trying to help a wounded soldier when he was shot in the back and his collarbone blown out. It was February 3, 1968, near a place called Hue. He lay there 13 hours surrounded by wounded and dead soldiers with intermittent gunfire all around him. Finally a beautiful black man braved the gunfire and pulled my husband to safety. (Thank you, sir, whoever you are.)

After a few days in the Philippines, George was shipped to Travis Air Force Base in California along with other seriously wounded soldiers. From there, they were put on a specially converted bus that had stretcher-beds instead of seats for the trip to Letterman Hospital in San Francisco.

Once there they were greeted by protesters. They were the "boys being brought home"—the ones the protesters supposedly wanted to come home safely.

Coming through the gate to the Presidio the bus was attacked by a crowd throwing rotten garbage and dirty baby diapers. The crowd called the wounded soldiers baby burners and child rapers. George tells of one soldier who pushed himself up on what little was left of his arms to see who was calling him a baby burner. The young man who had had his genitals blown off winced at being called a child raper. The crowd was nasty. They may have even spat on the bus. George didn't notice.

There were no "burly Green Berets" on this bus. My six-foot-one husband was down to 140 pounds, but he was in better shape than most of the others.

He recovered and drew the assignment of ambulance driver for military personnel and their dependents. He soon became accustomed to the daily crowd at the gates of the Presidio. Most just carried anti-war signs. Some yelled and made obscene gestures as he drove his military ambulance through.

Once in San Francisco, while George was picking up a diabetic who had lapsed into a coma, a crowd severely trashed his ambulance. He had to take his patient back inside so he could call the M.P.s. They came and held off the crowd so he could get his patient to the hospital.

Some of these things George had never told me about until right now. I wept. Some things are worse than being spat on.

CHARLES L. THUDIUM, PLAINFIELD, ILLINOIS

I am a Vietnam-era veteran who teaches high school and college in Du Page County, Illinois. I have never been spat upon but I had something happen to me that I would like to relate—it was in the same vein.

When I got out of the Army after serving three years, one

of which was spent in Asia, I entered Northeastern Illinois University to earn my teaching degree. The year was 1969 and at that point there were very few veterans at that particular institution.

During my first year at the college I had the unfortunate experience to take a sociology course taught by a very liberal professor. The first day of class we were told to give the standard oral biography that many teachers use to allow the class to get acquainted with each other.

After my turn the professor began to harass me about being part of the Army. From that day on he called me "Baby Killer." "Baby Killer" became my name to him. When he called on me that was the term he used. I took it for the entire course and never complained because I was young and this was my first college experience. I did not know that I probably could have protested to the department chairman.

Now with 15 years of teaching behind me I still find myself thinking about that man and the grief he caused me. Here was an educated man with multiple degrees in the social sciences, doing his best to make a young man feel bad. He used me to get back at a system he hated. I often wish that I could meet him again for a chat.

JOSEPH A. MCCALLISTER, SAN ANTONIO, TEXAS

I spent my tour of duty in the Central Highlands of Vietnam, from July 3, 1967 to August 2, 1968. When I returned to the States I was assigned to the Army National Guard duty station in Milwaukee, Wisconsin.

The day I arrived at the National Guard station—September 3, 1968—I had the desire to eat a pizza, so I went to a pizza parlor located close to a university. I entered the establishment dressed in my uniform and sat down at one of the tables. After I had waited for almost 15 minutes I called one of the waitresses to my table.

I started to give her my order and she said, "We don't serve pigs in uniform here. Get out."

I was so hurt and angry to be told this after going through hell in Vietnam. I left and reported to Headquarters. I told them what had happened, and I was told, "It happens all the time."

I retired from the service with 31 years of duty behind me. I was in World War II, Korea, and Vietnam. This incident will remain in my mind as the most insulting in my military career. They didn't throw urine in my face, but to me this was a lot worse.

JACK COUGHLIN, ORLAND PARK, ILLINOIS

Did we get spit on? You be the judge.

I came back to the world in late September 1968. As our plane approached San Francisco, we got our first look at what we all missed so very much—"The American Way of Life": rock and roll, round-eyed girls, fast cars, and good times. We were happy, real happy. We were only kids. We did our best, and we were home.

There were people protesting at the airport gates with signs and slurs directed at us. We made our way past the protesters to the first restroom we came to, where we exchanged our uniforms for civilian clothes. The sight of all those once-proud young American soldiers taking off their uniforms before traveling to their hometowns will stay with me forever.

There were only two types of people when I came home—those actively against what we did and those who said nothing. I spent the next 17 years saying nothing. I had no one to talk to.

JOHN C. HINCHLIFFE, JR., STAFFORD SPRINGS, CONNECTICUT

Nineteen seventy-two. University of Connecticut student union cafeteria. Last two years of college, just back (April) from Vietnam.

While rummaging through my Physics notes and sipping a cup of coffee, a young girl, perhaps nineteen or so (I was married, age twenty-four, former combat medic with the Army), remarked about my fatigue jacket, which I was wearing as she sat down at my table.

"Wow!" she said. "Cool jacket! Did you get it at——'s Surplus?"

Noting her unkempt appearance and manner, I replied, "No. From my uncle."

"Was he in the Army or something?" the girl asked.

I answered, "My Uncle Sam. I was in the Army."

"Were you in Vietnam?" she queried.

I proudly answered, "Yes."

She sat up, threw her coffee in my face, and left, after asking, "Did you bayonet any babies?"

A Navy vet in a pea coat immediately came over to my table and we chatted. This was October 1972. My wife was four months pregnant. I'm still angered by this incident. I know of no similar incidents among my friends.

STEPHEN D. NAGY, CHICAGO, ILLINOIS

In November 1969, while on leave before going to Vietnam, I was referred to as being a hired killer by a close relative (female), who was home from college and going through a radical phase at the time. This happened more than once.

On February 12, 1971, after my separation from the Army, I was chatting with a young lad between eleven and fourteen years old, who upon seeing my uniform asked me if I had just come back from Vietnam. After my affirmative response he asked me if I had carried a machine gun while I was there, and after I indicated I had he asked me how many babies I had shot with it. He seemed really disappointed to find out that I had been a Convoy Escort Military Policeman and hadn't had to shoot anyone. This occurred at San Francisco International Airport.

These were not "spitting incidents," but I might as well have been spat upon. You see, it wasn't only "hippies" and it wasn't just spitting. What happened was an attitude against not only the government and the generals but also the men—suckers, we were called—who went over to Nam and tried to do a job.

I'm sorry about the handwriting. I cried after the first draft and I am ready to now.

RUTLEDGE E. ETHERIDGE, JR., EAST LONGMEADOW, MASSACHUSETTS

My own experience in Vietnam was highly unusual. I was in the Submarine Service for four years (1966–1970). As you know, the Submarine Service is the Silent Service: "The boats are quiet; the men are mute."

It was my obligation then, as it remains now, to keep to myself details of submarine operations (where, when, how, etc.). This is not difficult now; the urge to "bare it all" withers with time and maturity. But in 1970, I had a strong story to tell. And the hostility and ignorance I encountered led me to want to tell it, all the more.

In 1970, I had just spent four years as part of a superbly trained, highly intelligent and motivated group of professionals. We "daring undersea raiders" were, and remain, true believers. None of us relished the carnage in Southeast Asia, as was commonly, incessantly charged. All of us truly believed that American involvement in the area was to stem

Communism, and to prevent a blood bath involving millions of victims.

When I enrolled at the University of Massachusetts at Amherst in January 1971, I had just turned twenty-one. More than 99 percent of my classmates had spent the previous four years in high school—hearing daily of the bloodshed, often and forcefully depicted as American-inspired atrocities perpetrated against a "local liberation" movement. Most of my classmates were eighteen, high-spirited, and knew everything.

I expected, under the circumstances, a culture clash; I was right. I thought I was prepared to deal with it; I was wrong.

I lived on the top floor of a 22-story dormitory (JFK Dorm). My roommate was an eighteen-year-old kid from eastern Massachusetts. He believed, as did many others, that Chairman Mao and Ho Chi Minh were Divinely appointed to save mankind from American Imperialism. My room was thus festooned with the usual props: posters of Mao and the Chicago Seven, little red booklets strewn around like chaff, etc. (I came to despise rock music during this time; my ears had survived four years of "pressure-slams" in the Submarine Service, but could not endure the blaring, disharmonic blathering of hard rock. I also developed a loathing for drug abuse, for which I have remained grateful.)

My roommate, and many others, made a point of "tolerating" me. I was called a child killer a few times (always from a distance), but most of my classmates seemed ready to forgive, and understand. It became, I think, a sign of liberal maturity to forgive, understand, and tolerate; as long as Vietnam veterans kept quiet, were contrite, and made no attempt to poison anyone else's mind.

(It's amazing and unsettling, how much old anger returns, and swells up, as I write this; this is my fourth attempt to write this letter so far.)

If it seems that my perceptions of attitudes were incorrect, or exaggerated, let me relate one (of many) incidents that occurred at UMass:

Because I felt a desire, perhaps need, to be understood, I wrote a two-page article about American involvement in Vietnam, outlining as well as I could the issues involved. I took the article to an on-campus group of fellow veterans, and rewrote it, to incorporate many different perspectives. (Many of the vets were opposed to our involvement in the war, and their viewpoints were important; they'd been there.)

I then took the article to the student union office of the campus newspaper, and asked that it be published. I was told the article, now three pages, was too long. (The previous two issues of the newspaper had each contained articles much longer.) I condensed, rewrote, and resubmitted the article twice before giving up.

My next move was to make (at my own expense) 500 copies of the article. With three other vets, I began passing the copies out, near the building site of the library. As was always the case, there were several other groups around, passing out their own literature. We stayed there for about an hour; the passing students accepted the literature and moved on. After a while a shouting match developed between us and other students. When rocks were thrown at us, we left. (One of the guys with me was an ex-SEAL; I was more concerned about the safety of the rock throwers than I was about ours. But I was frightened, and more, I think, just plain shocked.)

When I returned to my dorm, a message was waiting for me. My belongings—books, bedding, clothes, and personal items—had been piled in the hallway outside my room. A fresh coat of red spray paint (to symbolize blood) had been liberally applied. Over my bed, "Fashist" (misspelled) and "Pig Scum" had been sprayed on the wall.

There were other incidents that stick in my craw, and in my memory, but I think that one brought into play all the attitudes (including mine) that contributed to the conflicts I encountered on campus.

Despite the anger that sometimes wells up, I consider the experience, from a personal perspective, as having been positive. I have never regretted my years in the Submarine Service; I met extraordinary people, and developed values, which I shall never forget. The adversity, during and after my years at sea, has strengthened me, and allowed me to think from many points of view. And, of course, there was a lot of good that came from my years at UMass.

But I would be less than honest if I did not admit that a lot of it hurt, very deeply, at the time.

RON LA GARDY, PRAIRIE VIEW, ILLINOIS

After a year in Vietnam with the 44th Medical Brigade, I returned to the United States in April 1967. After I was processed out of Oakland I was taken to the airport for a flight home.

While still in uniform I tried to get a ticket to Chicago at three different airlines' reservations desks and was told there were no seats available on any flight home. I told them I did not have to fly standby, that I would pay full coach fare because I just wanted to get home, but that didn't make any difference. They said there were no seats.

I decided to change out of uniform in the men's room to see if that would make a difference. As I was walking by, people stopped and stared at me as if I was not welcome, and many made derogatory comments to me.

After I changed my clothes I went back to the ticket counter and what do you think—sure enough, all of a sudden there was a seat available for me back to Chicago. As far as I was concerned, that was as much a spit in the face as a direct hit from someone's mouth. Even now it still hurts and feels like it was just yesterday that it happened.

ELLEN RANCK, WHEATON, ILLINOIS

I am jolted into remembering the humiliation I felt for my combat soldier beau (now husband). Fred was infantry, 101st Airborne, and he had a month's leave in December 1969 before his second tour in Nam.

He arrived at O'Hare Airport in Chicago and decided to spend several days downtown. I picked what I thought was the best hotel for his stay.

The reservations desk clerk told Fred, who was in uniform and well decorated, that the hotel didn't want him there. She said that they had had trouble with other Nam soldiers. I asked how they could be so discriminatory to someone who was serving his country. She spoke to her supervisor, and they decided that Fred could have a room . . . if he paid all three days' lodging in advance and in cash.

I asked if they required prepayment from all their patrons. I gave them my business card, and finally they waived the prepay.

We went to dinner in the hotel's steak house, and were placed at the worst table there (with many other tables empty). Our waiter repeatedly ignored us. We drank and had a leisurely dinner. As we were ready to leave, the waiter grabbed Fred and told him the tip was inadequate. If that waiter had any idea as to Fred's combat record, I'm certain he would not have approached Fred.

I guess I should have silenced the waiter. But instead, Fred quietly paid him what he wanted, turned to me, and asked, "Why doesn't anyone respect me as a U.S. soldier? I'm only doing the job they gave me to do."

I will always feel sad that Fred did not get the soldier's welcome he so richly deserved when he first came back to America. And after all these years, I am sending a copy of this letter to the hotel.

CHARLES F. CORSON, BOULDER, COLORADO

I'm a Vietnam veteran (May 1968-May 1969). Having spent six months stationed in the northern California area prior to going to Vietnam, I had come into contact with "hippies" and "peaceniks" and, indeed, grooved on the San Francisco-Berkeley scene at that time.

However, I was totally unprepared for the "reception" when I returned from Nam to "the world." Although no one ever spat at me with saliva, there were those who spat the word baby killer, murderer, and worse when I came through the airports in Seattle and San Francisco in May 1969.

Pretty weird for a young (twenty-two) GI getting back, hoping to get his discharge from the military after four-and-a-half years and hoping to get back into civilian clothes, enjoy life, and maybe get into college. I wasn't sure how I would fit into an America that had changed a lot.

One day I'm in Pleiku and the rockets are exploding. In two days I'm at an Air Force base in the state of Washington getting processed out, and then I'm on my way to the Seattle airport to catch a plane to visit some friends for a couple of days to readjust myself before flying home to Philadelphia to see my Mom, my Dad, and my brothers. Both airports, I'm called names.

Because my hair was fairly short, I was easily picked out as a GI, even when I was in civilian clothes. The taunts hurt. I heard them on the West Coast and on the East Coast when I returned there.

Couple this with running into a right-wing ideologue from my high school class at a bar one night, with him ranting on about how he supports the war and why we should bomb the "gooks" into oblivion, but not listening to me relate that the farmers caught in the middle of the war, the ones who suffered the most, didn't have an interest in the ideological conflict.

Hell, it was pretty complex. Pretty sad. No wonder I went into a shell for years.

ALLEN D. MOHR, MOLINE, ILLINOIS

I enlisted in the United States Marine Corps on April 16, 1967, and landed in Vietnam on September 27, 1967. I participated in at least 10 major operations and countless patrols, ambushes, etc. I came back to the world on October 15, 1968.

There were no demonstrations either at my departure or return, but the fact that we left for Vietnam around 4 a.m. and returned at 2 a.m. in October of 1968 may have had something to do with that. I felt like we were being snuck back into the country.

No one ever actually spat upon me. If they had—yes, I would have torn them apart. But here are some things that did happen to me.

One of the first things someone asks you upon learning you were in Vietnam is, "Did you kill anyone?" If they only knew what a personal question that is, maybe they wouldn't ask. I used to just lower my head and ignore them, but recently I look them in the eye and say yes I have. If they are seriously interested in my experiences I will spend the time to explain what happened and why.

One woman couldn't understand that if I didn't kill the North Vietnamese soldiers they would have killed me or my friends. In 1971, while sitting in a bar at a table away from the other patrons, I was having a beer with two other ex-Marines. We were quietly discussing the war. Our discussion was not about violence, just about some humorous incidents that had happened to us overseas. A janitor was evidently listening to our discussion. All of a sudden he started screaming "Murderers, murderers, baby killers" and pointing in our direction.

When I went back to college at Southern Illinois University in 1971 I was—or at least I felt like—the only hawk on campus. One day I ran into a ''friend'' I had known there before I went into the service. He seemed genuinely glad to see me and asked what I'd been doing. I told him I had been in the Marines and in Vietnam. He looked at me like I was dirt and said, ''What a sucker.'' Maybe I was a sucker, but not a coward.

Mr. Mohr's recounting of the actions of the janitor is representative of a subtle, but important, point that runs through many of these stories: that when people were abusive to the returning veterans, those people often chose to make a public display of their abusive behavior. Apparently it wasn't enough to make some private, pointed gesture to a soldier—the people who were acting cruelly felt a compulsion to do it in a setting that would call others' attention to the act.

Part of this, of course, might be attributed to cowardice— it's easier to harass someone when there are other people around who you know are likely to support your viewpoint. Some veterans whose stories have appeared here have offered the opinion that the crowds of airport spitters and shouters were part of an organized group—perhaps a national group. Certainly the anti-war movement was national in scale, but it is unlikely that all of these unpleasant encounters were being meticulously coordinated. It makes more sense to consider the fact that people who would spit at, or verbally taunt, a returning soldier would find safety in outnumbering that soldier, or small group of soldiers.

Putting that aside for a moment, though, the story of the janitor in the bar adds resonance to the fact that just at the time when many returning veterans wanted only to be left alone and to fade into the background for a few months, some of them were involuntarily pushed into the public spot-

light—even when the spotlight was in as small a setting as a
tavern. Whoever that janitor was, he has probably forgotten
about the whole incident by now, even as Mr. Mohr remem-
bers it so vividly all these years later. Multiply it by all the
other public incidents and it explains quite a bit of pain.

STEPHEN R. FRANK, SEPULVEDA, CALIFORNIA

The question about the treatment of Vietnam vets returning home hit me through the heart.

I served with the First Infantry Division in Vietnam from
the end of January 1968 until the end of August 1968. After
traveling half a day to get to Saigon to leave country, another
day completing my papers to get out of the country and another three-fourths of a day traveling, I finally made it to a
base outside of Oakland, California to be released from the
Army. Because my paperwork was not completed until late
in the evening, my first night back in the United States was
spent trying to sleep (after having been awake three straight
days) in a chair in the Oakland airport.

I took the first flight on Sunday, the day before Labor Day,
1968, to Los Angeles to get home to my family. After arriving at about 9 or 10 in the morning (after all these years it is
difficult to remember the actual arrival time) my parents took
me to my favorite restaurant on Fairfax Boulevard.

Besides my mother and father, my thirteen-year-old sister
was also with us. As we got to the restaurant, my father took
the car, with my mother inside, and went to park.

While he was parking the car my sister and I walked up
the street to the entrance of the restaurant to get a table. Since
I had just gotten out of the Army the night before, I still had
on my uniform.

As we approached the entrance of the restaurant, some

long-haired smelly creature approached me, used profanity, called me a murderer of children, and wanted me to fight him. The words used by this piece of filth were the same used on the battlefield.

No, I was not spat upon. It was worse—in front of my thirteen-year-old sister to be called a murderer of children, profane names, and an individual who—to quote the intruder—"should have died in Vietnam."

One does not need to be hit to be hurt.

JAMES W. WAGENBACH, GOLDEN, COLORADO

Upon returning from Vietnam in 1968 minus my right arm, I was accosted twice—once on the campus of the University of Denver and once at the University of Colorado.

On both occasions I was in uniform and approached by student-type individuals who inquired, "Where did you lose your arm? Vietnam?"

I replied, "Yes."

The response was, "Good. Serves you right."

JOHN L. BARRETT, AURORA, COLORADO

I received a gunshot wound in Vietnam in September 1968, and on my return home in late October I was required to change planes and airlines at Chicago's O'Hare Airport. I was on crutches and wearing a full leg cast. I was also trying to carry a travel bag, which was rather difficult, as I was inexperienced on crutches.

A pair of college-age males walked up on either side of me and one of them asked if I was returning from Vietnam. I replied that I was, and they asked a couple more questions about my injury and acted very friendly. Suddenly they kicked my crutches out from under me, pointed and laughed at me on the floor, then took off running.

This left a lasting impression on me and from then on I knew that going to college with this type around me was out of the question. I was positive that I would end up hurting someone.

Although I remember this experience very vividly, what I remember more is the concern and help that I received from other people who witnessed the incident. Especially the older couple from Mount Prospect, Illinois, who not only carried my bag to my departure gate, but even offered to drive me to my home in South Bend, Indiana.

In the 20 years since that incident I have realized feelings in both directions, but the majority has been favorable. And it has improved immensely in the last five years or so. I am sure that most Nam vets realize that it was a small minority that caused them the trouble and grief.

CHUCK WAGNER, GREEN BAY, WISCONSIN

When I returned in October 1971, my plane landed at Oakland Air Base at 3 a.m. Not many protesters were up at that hour. After processing out of the service I took a cab over to San Francisco airport for a flight to Green Bay.

My plane wasn't leaving for another few hours so I passed the time with a little reading. A guy came over and struck up a conversation. He kept pestering me to go to his apartment where he had a great stereo setup. He said we'd pick up a couple of girls and have a party.

It took me about two hours to shake this guy. When he excused himself to go to the men's room, I took off, only to be stopped by a man in a suit, showing me his shield and I.D. He said that he was a special agent of the FBI, and that another agent and himself had been following the guy who had been bothering me. He was suspected of attacking, beating, robbing, and molesting Vietnam vets upon returning from Nam. The guy was arrested.

When I got on the plane, a woman in the seat across the aisle got up and moved, saying she wouldn't sit next to a baby killer.

I had just spent one year, eight months, and 11 days trying to serve my country to the best of my ability. All in all, it was a real "nice" welcome home.

MICHAEL A. HOUSE, EAST TAUNTON, MASSACHUSETTS

As a twice-wounded Vietnam veteran (medic), I was not spat upon, but harassed in other ways. One example was when I had an overnight liberty after getting out of the hospital, so I thought I would take advantage of it to see some of the beautiful sights of San Francisco.

I became the center of a violent argument between two groups in the middle of the sidewalk. One group was calling me a killer, while the other group was arguing that I was doing my job.

Being called a killer has stuck in my memory for many years, particularly since my job was to save lives. My only weapon in Nam was a .45-caliber pistol for self-defense and defense of my patients.

SUSAN T. MELVILLE, KIRKLAND, WASHINGTON

I spent six years in Vietnam with the Agency for International Development. When I returned I attended a land grant college (not a hotbed of war resistance), then went to work for a major chemical company.

I was speaking to a group about the use in local forests of the chemical which is now known as Agent Orange, and I mentioned having lived in Vietnam. A woman jumped on a table and started yelling that I was a baby killer. I was amazed at her behavior because I knew very little about the anti-war activities in the U.S. (Armed Forces TV had rather limited news coverage on this subject.) Had I been a vet, my reaction would have undoubtedly been different.

Second story—I have a friend who works for a local government agency and has a staff of approximately 20. He didn't start the job until three years after Saigon fell. Some time ago I remember him saying he would not hire a Vietnam vet because they were all murderers.

Spit on? Seems to me that's pretty mild stuff. At least the uniformed Green Berets in the airports could retaliate. How do the vets retaliate who live with the kind of people I have described?

MICHAEL T. LAMBRIGHT, MANSFIELD, OHIO

During my first semester (Fall 1975) as a journalism major at Northern Arizona University, I had an introductory Mass Communications media class. The instructor's discussion topic for one of the class sessions was: "The Media War—Vietnam." On that day, the instructor asked the class whether or not there were any Vietnam veterans in attendance. One individual and myself answered affirmatively. The instructor then requested that we share our Vietnam insights during the ensuing discussion.

Approximately 15 minutes into this class discussion, a just-out-of-high-school male student raised his hand and directed the following question at the other veteran and myself: "How is it that you two can live with yourselves knowing that you are attending this university on that GI Bill blood money?"

This literally stunned the other veteran and myself speechless. We hadn't even had the opportunity to recover and retort when the majority of the 50 or so students in that classroom started chiming in with questions of a similar vein, or statements supporting the young man's perspective.

The instructor had to literally shut down the class to regain control. He then offered the other veteran and myself an opportunity to reply. The other veteran chose to remain silent—he was obviously angry and informed me afterwards that he had been on the verge of losing his self-control. I opted to make a statement to the class that: ''You have been force-fed, by the government and the media, misinformation on Vietnam—you really don't know of what you are insinuating.'' The other veteran and I then packed up our books and left.

You don't have to be physically spat upon as a Vietnam veteran to be cognizant of the American ''majority's'' entrenched prejudicial and discriminatory attitudes on Vietnam and that war's veterans. It's a daily fact of life in a myriad of formats, ranging from blatant to indiscreet. And all the homecoming parades, positive veteran media events such as ''Platoon,'' Vietnam memorials, and supportive political rhetoric—from now until hell freezes over—will not ever truly affect such an ingrained, entrenched public attitude.

DON WOODWARD, BIRMINGHAM, ALABAMA

In May 1970 I arrived in California after one year in Vietnam. I had been advised not to wear jungle boots, fatigues, or medals. I didn't. I was also lucky enough to come back to the States via Tokyo and land at a military base.

However, three days later, I walked into a bar and asked an American girl—the first I had seen—if I could buy her a drink. She said, ''Go fuck yourself, baby killer.'' To this day I don't know how she knew I was from Vietnam.

I didn't kill anybody. I worked in an office.

JERRY OLSON, OAKHAM, MASSACHUSETTS

I spent 601 days in South Vietnam, exclusive of leave and R&R time, between late August 1968 and April 1970. I cannot honestly say to you that I was spat upon by any civilians because I had done time in Nam (although as an M.P., I'd been spat on and spat at by a number of irate GIs whose fun it was, regrettably, my job to spoil).

But I was hassled at an airport on my way to the Nam. I had orders to report to the Oakland Army Terminal for overseas processing about a week before August ended. My brother, my brother-in-law, and a drunken Marine lieutenant we had picked up along the way saw me off from Boston. My recollection is that it was a Sunday. I landed at O'Hare in Chicago, where I would have a three or four hour layover waiting for my connector flight to San Francisco, sometime between 10 and midnight. I bought a magazine and a pack of cigarettes and sat at the appropriate gate to wait for my flight.

For a while, I was all alone. Maybe 40 minutes later, I was joined by some young folks my age (I was twenty at the time), who were apparently waiting for somebody to arrive. I wouldn't call them hippies, although they were long-haired, certainly by contrast to my GI coif. Their conversation was replete with the jargon of the day, and one of them sported peace symbols galore. Eventually, I got drawn into their conversation, sitting there khaki-clad and Nam-bound.

When I mentioned that last fact, they forthwith jumped in my shit, and rambled on about that being what they were in Chicago to protest. As I said, nobody spat at me or put me in any kind of physical danger, but I was called things you can't print. I was a kid, stuck in a strange city for a few hours on his way to war, scared and already homesick.

Sometime later a large Chicago police officer (I'll never forget his checkered cap) strolled over and put his hand on my shoulder. He had apparently been observing us for some time. I looked up at him and when I did he asked, "These people bothering you, Olson?" He must have read my name tag. I either nodded or creaked out an affirmative, after which this cop said to my tormentors—again, in words you couldn't print—go away and leave the soldier alone.

They did—he was damn hard to ignore—and the policeman asked me when my flight was. I told him. He said, "Follow me," which I did. He led me to one of those small bars in one of the O'Hare concourses, and said to the bartender, "Take care of this guy, will ya?" Wisely, the bartender agreed to take care of me—about seven Lowenbraus, as I recall, till my flight to San Francisco a few hours hence.

Some weeks later, after I had helped quell a riot myself (at LBJ, the stockade at Long Binh to which I'd been assigned as a prison guard), I got hold of a copy of Newsweek, in which the Chicago police were taken to task at the Democratic convention. It may be that both my tormentors and my rescuer met again that week.

The idea of hippies spitting on "a burly member of the Green Berets" fresh from a tour of duty fighting the North Vietnamese in the bush isn't an accurate description. Just as everybody who opposed the war wasn't a hippie, the typical guy coming back from Nam wasn't a Green Beanie. Most weren't even grunts in the bush. They were rear echelon motherfuckers—ammo humpers, or finance clerks, medics. Maybe they worked in supply or were M.P.s. Not much in their Nam experience would condition them to do anything but "stand there and take it," because for a full year, that's just what they did. They stood there and took it—from colonels, captains, sergeants—even if they never raised an M16 against a VC. For a lot of guys, the enemy had been the Army, not the Nam, and being hassled at the airport in uniform, while unwelcome, was often the last act of harassment in their military careers.

MICHAEL E. DOYLE, DENVER, COLORADO

Spat upon? No. Ribbons torn from my blouse, mustard sprayed on my uniform? Yes.

I served as a U.S. Marine from 1967 to 1968 as an enlisted man, senior staff NCO, and as an officer. I am a disabled veteran and have begun to experience the long-term effects of my service.

My first experience with a "welcome home" committee was upon my return from Vietnam following the Tet Offensive. I was one of four individuals from my platoon who came home at the end of a 13-month tour. Our friends had died or been wounded badly enough so as not to return to combat. Upon arriving home in Denver my parents explained to me how they did not want me to discuss my experiences with my younger brothers for fear of injuring them emotionally. My brothers were eighteen, fifteen, and seven at that time; I was nineteen.

Following a Sunday Mass at which the priest preached on the immorality of the war, and a verbal assault at a restaurant by persons who interrupted my family's breakfast to make sure I understood their message, my parents asked me not to wear my uniform in public. Upon returning from leave I volunteered to return to Vietnam.

My second return to the U.S. was in 1970, when I came home on a Medevac flight. Later that year a family from San Clemente won me as their dinner guest for Thanksgiving. While the gentleman and his wife were extremely gracious, their children had found reasons why they would not attend the Thanksgiving dinner. The ride back to the hospital was one of the longest of my life.

Following the Thanksgiving outing, the city of Burbank and Disneyland sponsored a welcome home party for Vietnam veterans. The town fed us at an outdoor shopping mall and then transported us to Disneyland where the staff and a majority of the crowd went out of their way to make us feel special and welcome. While waiting in line for a haunted house ride, we were greeted by a small group of individuals who ripped our ribbons and badges from our blouses and sprayed mustard onto us. The cowardice of this act is appreciated if you realize we had been lectured to do nothing to disgrace the Marine Corps, and all the Marines and Navy Corpsmen in my group were on crutches, using walkers, or wearing braces.

What I haven't discussed were the incidents in airports and in stores where adults would shout at my children that their father was a Nazi and a baby killer as we walked from the grocery store to the car with the milk my wife had asked me to pick up.

I hope everybody quickly builds all the local memorials to the Vietnam veterans, and I hope everybody who wants to "welcome home" a Vietnam veteran has the chance. Then I hope they leave us alone.

BONNIE STOJAN, CLARE, ILLINOIS

I am the wife of a Vietnam veteran. We got married a week after he returned from Vietnam in 1968. I think the word for America's treatment of the veterans is "shunned."

My husband got back to the States and landed in Seattle. Before he returned home, he was told to put on civilian clothes for his own safety. Fortunately he came in at 3 a.m. (in uniform) and there weren't any protesters.

However, I can remember going out and if we were to go into bars and people found out he had been in Nam we would usually end up leaving because there would be trouble. After all the fighting my husband went through, it wasn't worth his time to argue with someone who hadn't been there.

And yes, the veterans took it! I think it was beneath their dignity to argue with the protesters, when deep down most of the protesters were just plain "chicken" to go. I think the returning vets were just damn glad to be home and alive, and the old "sticks and stones" theory worked easier than fighting. Those that did fight back were considered troublemakers. It was a "no win" situation.

My husband joined a chapter of Vietnam veterans, and it has been the most satisfying thing he has ever done. Together they are getting the pride back. The "Welcome Home Parade" in Chicago was the greatest day of our lives.

D. M. GONZALEZ, WHEELING, ILLINOIS

My hitch was up in early 1968, just before the Tet Offensive. I got the hell out of the Navy and returned home to Tampa, Florida to return to college. Being a strapping twenty-two-year-old, six-foot-one, 185-pound man, no one was going to spit on me!

I found, however, a very strong anti-war sentiment gripping the Clearwater campus of Saint Petersburg Junior College. Not only were the students caught up in the anti-war hysteria, a twenty-three-year-old female instructor was an avowed anarchist and faculty adviser to the local chapter of SDS [Students for a Democratic Society]. This organization, under her guidance, was given carte blanche by the college administration. Consequently, they were allowed to sponsor a "moratorium day observance" against the war.

During the moratorium day observance, punctuated by speeches from self-styled anti-war activists and professional protesters from off campus, I was denounced as a "fascist," a "baby killer," and a "war criminal." I was repeatedly and vociferously berated for my "crimes against the Vietnamese people" while being force-fed harangues extolling the sainthood of Ho Chi Minh.

In Vietnam I had flown with a photo-recon squadron, and had three buddies vaporized out of the sky next to me as we flew an intelligence mission over Southeast Asia. (The enemy gunner could just as easily have aimed at my aircraft.) I'm not proud of the fact that I let these know-nothings on campus get to me, but the fact is that I experienced indignation bordering on rage. My buddies had given their lives to protect the liberties of these ingrates, and I was now being subjected to their collective vitriol. Baby killer, indeed!

No, I didn't bash them, I did the only thing I could do: I joined the Young Americans for Freedom and the Young Republicans, went to work as a policeman, and finally returned to the military service, from which I'll retire in two years.

PETE S. JUSSEL, SANTA CRUZ, CALIFORNIA

No being spit on. Just angry questions from a woman in an airport bar in Philadelphia. Like, "What are you doing over there? Killing kids?" and shit like that. I was alone, she was with a group. The rest of her group looked on in silence. It was August, 1968.

I later deserted and moved to Canada, where I lived (Ottawa) for five years, then came back, got an undesirable discharge, and moved out to California. I'm a family man now.

DAVID H. KLINE, LITTLETON, COLORADO

My background: Twenty years in the United States Marine Corps (master sergeant, retired August 1980), Vietnam veteran (March 1967-December 1968). I was never spat upon. My story is different, and the pain is still inside, just like it was yesterday.

The incident that turned me inside out happened on a Friday during summer school at Palomar Junior College in 1972. I was in uniform. The English class was called "Word

Study,'' and was taught by a woman in her late forties or early fifties.

I was sitting near the front of the class, taking notes on the lecture. About halfway through the class, the teacher turned from the blackboard and her discussion, stepped up to the front row of students, and pointed at me.

"How many babies did you kill in Vietnam?" was her statement. Frustrated, I took my books and left. The incident was personal, but has had a profound effect on my life and attitude. Although I stuck out 20 years because I can justify an armed forces, I can't justify the war or the forces controlling it, even today.

My advice to my sons, nephews, and nieces is go to school and try to become powerful, don't volunteer for the service, and if drafted go to another country.

JAMES C. O'NEIL, JR., SIERRA VISTA, ARIZONA

At six feet five and 210 pounds, I would have fought back if anyone had spat at me. I was, however, sneered at, ugly comments were made, and people spat on the ground in a derogatory manner. New York's Kennedy Airport was the worst place for me, and that was March 1969.

The worst incident I have direct knowledge of occurred in Williamsburg, Virginia. A widow lost her only son in Vietnam, and when the obituary was published a group of students held a demonstration in front of her house. They burned an American flag—called her son a baby killer—and made what was already a tragedy into a despicable horror.

I have not yet been able to forget or forgive that. I fought for everyone's right to disagree openly, but not for the "right" to hurt or deprive others of comfort and dignity for their beliefs, however unpopular. Napalm would have been too quick for that despicable group—it is well that I was not there, for I still feel no mercy.

Lest this seem all bad, there were people who voiced support, went out of their way for us, told us about their experiences, etc. The people of Effingham, Illinois and Darwin, Australia, deserve special thanks for their support of the soldiers.

ANTHONY N. STANFA, CHICAGO, ILLINOIS

I left combat duty in Vietnam in July 1968, returned home, and the first question I was asked by a friend was, "How many people did you kill?" From that day on, I buried the past year, for I knew "they can't possibly understand." Forty-eight hours earlier, 10,000 miles away, putting friends on Medevac choppers—no, the people back home didn't understand.

I started attending the Central YMCA College in January 1969. Nearly every day the lobby was filled with tables displaying anti-war material and armbands to protest our "killing of women and children" in Vietnam.

When handed the material, I took it and later threw it away. Nearly every male student there was enrolled so he would not get drafted. They let it be known. I had been going to school on weekdays, but I switched classes as soon as possible to all-day Saturday—the students on Saturdays were adults.

It hurt a lot, thinking about too many friends that I lost. Today I still have the flashbacks, crying for my friends and their families. I have visited many graves, and met many families.

In one case (this was in 1984) as I spoke to my deceased buddy's parents, the mother just listened and smiled. Finally, the father took me outside and told me his wife is still waiting for her son to come home. She thinks he is alive.

Apparently when both parents were notified of his death, the mother had a breakdown and ended up in a hospital. She never attended the services and has never gone to the cemetery "because her son is not dead." Other than that, she works every day and is perfect.

The list goes on. I marched in the "Welcome Home" parade, and my family loved it. It was too late, the damage was done and over.

JOHN M. MOLTZ, JR., COPPERAS COVE, TEXAS

I served in the Army throughout the Vietnam war. I spent two tours in Nam and hence returned to the U.S.A. twice from Vietnam. During the same period I also served a tour in Korea during which I returned on leave at mid-tour and at the end of the tour. Of course, civilians only knew I was returning from the Far East, but not where. Additionally, from 1968 to 1970 I served, in uniform, as a member of the ROTC faculty of a major Eastern university.

I always found air terminal workers and flight attendants to be courteous and understanding. They were simply super. The adverse comments that were made came mostly from student-age young people. On commercial flights, I had several conversations with adult passengers which more resembled inquiries into what was really happening in Vietnam than support or criticism of the war.

My tour with ROTC was violent. In the first place, there were only a few of us on a large campus. We were not armed and we were vastly outnumbered. Most campus administrators, faculty, and students were supportive and genuinely curious about what was happening. However, as is well-known worldwide, some students were radical, outspoken, and violent. This group was frustrated because they did not represent even close to a majority and yet they just KNEW that they were right and they needed to change the world to their way of thinking. These folks took their wrath out on

ROTC cadets, ROTC buildings, and military personnel in uniform.

As a member of the Army's speakers bureau, I went out to speak to a large number of civic groups. My observation was that the vast majority of people were supportive of our efforts, and although they may have had some reservations as to the wisdom of our either being in the conflict or how it was being fought, they did not blame the soldier for that. They viewed him as a sort of victim caught in the middle. Violence came from a select few students and in isolated incidents.

I do not for a moment regret the 22 years I served my country. I feel a sadness and frustration for the millions of people we abandoned in Vietnam. No, most of us were not spat upon when we came home, but it hurts to remember those who died to help hopeless people on behalf of a nation that—in the last analysis, by its withdrawal—proved it didn't give a damn.

ELAINE DAVIES, OCEANSIDE, CALIFORNIA

I am in the process of retiring after 28 years of Marine Corps service. I am retiring as a colonel, although I served in Vietnam while I was a captain/major, from May 1968 to May 1969. Although I was not spat upon, I was showered with raw eggs on my return to the United States.

I was the second woman Marine Corps officer to be ordered to Vietnam. I was a volunteer, and although I would not change the opportunity to have served there, I probably would not have volunteered to remain beyond the one-year tour.

Since my case was rather unique (being a woman in Vietnam), it was customary for the Marine Corps to debrief the returnee in Washington, D.C. I had returned in the early part of May 1969 and had been ordered to my new duty station in California. I was in California long enough to say hello to my parents, and then proceeded to Washington. My mother had driven me to the Los Angeles airport, had dropped me at the proper terminal, and had not remained with me while I waited to board my flight. I was happy that she did not have to witness what happened to me during my short wait in the terminal.

I was in uniform, and I did wear the ribbons indicating Vietnam service. I always carried extra uniforms in a carry-on hanging bag, as I never trusted anyone else to ensure that I arrived at my destination with sufficient uniforms for wear during my temporary duty period.

As a result, I had my hands full with my handbag, a hanging bag, and reading material. I was early, but I reported to the clerk at the desk so that I could get a window seat. As I walked into the waiting area, a commotion caught my attention. A rather large group of young people had vaulted over the rails that separated the waiting area for my flight from the other flight waiting areas. And, to my surprise, they were headed toward me. I tried to find a place to put my gear on a chair, but before I could empty my hands, a very tall, well-built, physically dirty young man (I would have guessed in his late teens or early twenties), with long, unkempt hair, took a raw egg and rubbed its broken contents over my left breast pocket where my ribbons were located.

To say that I was in shock was an understatement. First of all, anyone who would dare touch me in that area without my permission usually ended up with retaliation to some vital organ or spot near and dear to the toucher's sensitivities. I had been back in the United States for about a week by that time, and was still in cultural shock, so my reflexes were not at their sharpest. The first thing that came to mind was that I must change into a clean uniform—I was terribly embarrassed for being seen in such a state. Not much was said during this assault, except that I was called baby killer and several names that questioned my sexual preference and my heritage. Additionally, I was demeaned for having been stupid enough and gutless enough to have served in Vietnam.

Still in somewhat of a state of shock, I walked away from this group of male and female children, and headed for the ladies' room as a rather large crowd began to gather. I changed into a clean uniform, rolled the eggy one into a ball, and placed it in a plastic bag supplied by a very nice elderly lady who happened to be in the restroom when I went in to change. I walked back out into the waiting crowd—only to have the same creep repeat his act for still another group of watching people.

I had one clean uniform left in my hanging bag. I was astonished and somewhat bewildered that this stranger would seek me out to tantalize. First, I was female, second, I was very unceremonious about getting myself to the waiting area. And third, I did not react in the manner that I am sure they all expected. So, I unzipped the hanging bag and offered the clean uniform to the group to smear with egg, so that it would save me another trip to the ladies' room. They just disappeared. The whole group of them headed for the escalator and just disappeared.

I again went into the ladies' restroom, removed my dirty uniform, placed the second one in the plastic bag with the first one, and put on my third clean uniform. When I got back to the waiting area, my flight was about ready to board, and a group of older men and women rallied around to offer their sympathies.

Not once, while this had been happening, did anyone, male or female, step forward to offer assistance. In Vietnam we had all heard that things like this were common in our country. Even as it happened, I could not believe it was happening to me. I was rather shy about my status, and was not one to hurl myself into any situation where I might call attention to myself. In spite of the reputation for boisterousness in public, we were taught in training to act like ladies, especially when wearing the uniform. And this I did.

Many of the unpleasant incidents regarding Vietnam have been lost to memory, especially after all these years have passed. I am married to a wonderful gent who also served his country in Vietnam, and who has just retired after more than 30 years of active service.

But I cannot forget this!!!! I remember that 30 minutes of my life as if it happened just yesterday. I am about five feet two inches tall, and weighed about 120 pounds in those days. I guess the mystery of this tale is, what did they expect to gain? There weren't any police around at the time, so I couldn't yell for help. I didn't know the names of the people who were doing this to me, or the name of any group they may have been affiliated with, nor did they offer this information. If they were trying to demoralize a returning veteran, they did that to me, but they didn't know it.

I wonder if those people in the airport are still proud of the stance they took in those days? I am still ashamed of them, and I find it hard to see their side. That is what is wonderful about this country—one can believe one's own way. But I was violated, and whether or not you can believe my story is your choice. I have recovered, and I am probably a better person for the experience. But I cannot forget.

In spite of those of that generation and persuasion, I still was happy to have served my country. My scars can hardly be seen, but theirs will be with them forever. Semper Fidelis.

WILLIAM A. COMITO, KILLEEN, TEXAS

I was in a bar in San Francisco in 1968. I had been wounded in Vietnam and was convalescing at Letterman General Hospital at the Presidio. I went AWOL in my dress greens (the only clothes I had), and did some sightseeing with my arm in a sling. I was having a beer in a local bar when this long-haired type started making comments in my direction. He came over, leaned on my table, and got abusive.

One of his comments was something to the effect of, "How many innocent people have you killed?" I reached into my sling, pulled out a switchblade, flicked it open, and stuck it into the table about half an inch from his hand. I said, "Fifty-three," or some absurd number like that. I then asked him if he wanted to be the next. I didn't do much for Army P.R. but I was allowed to drink my beer in peace.

There are thousands of vets who never had the well-publicized problems of stress and flashbacks, if only for the reason that a very large percentage of Viet vets were never in combat per se. I am a Vietnam vet who was in ground combat as an enlisted man. I joined the Army in 1966 and re-upped in 1968. I spent two tours in Nam, got out and went to college, and came back in as an officer through ROTC. I had it better than most because I stayed in the military and did not suffer the culture shock of immediate return into a hostile society that many vets experienced. I have known many well-adjusted combat vets who were able to overcome their experience or hide it, and live normal lives.

Be that as it may, the U.S. government was wrong and the soldiers and ultimately future generations of Americans are victims of that war. Not victims in terms of death, disablement, trauma, or stress; but victims in terms of self-respect, commitment, volunteerism, the willingness to put community and nation ahead of self.

Yes, we are victims, and not because we were treated badly by our fellow citizens when we returned—they were motivated by the media and tarred us all with the same brush. The Army was as bad as any other employer in the way it treated vets.

I refuse to be made a victim. I did what I did because I thought that it was the right thing to do. I take responsibility for what I did, and refuse to feel guilty about the sins of omission and commission that were done by others.

LARRY F. PAULEY, GARDEN CITY, KANSAS

The "spitting" happened much less frequently than the cat-calls and total disrespect for a fellow human. The shouts of "butcher," "baby killer," "war monger," etc., were, for the most part, easier to take than the elbowing in line, stepping on your feet, or the intrusion upon your state of mind of "I'm home."

As for veterans "just standing there and taking it"—most of us, particularly in the early years, were too "shell shocked" and totally confused by our "Welcome Home" that we could not react. By the early Seventies you didn't dare try to react because they all "knew their rights" and then you caught the "double jeopardy" of civilian and military lawyers.

"The Wall" is not only a fitting tribute to the men whose names are on it, but also—and maybe more—to the 2 million minds that remember the pain, the terror, the fear, the agony of at least one name in particular. "Why" is probably the largest hurdle that we have to face. "Why" were we there? "Why" did we die? "Why" did we get treated like dogs on our return?

Got carried away. Like my cap says, "Vietnam Veteran and Proud of It."

DONALD ROMANCAK, WILLOWICK, OHIO

Having served in Vietnam from December 1968 to December 1969, I was discharged from Fort Ord. Upon my arrival at the airport for my flight home, and my first real contact with civilian surroundings, I found a seat next to a very pretty blonde girl, who certainly fit the "hippie" type.

After just getting seated next to her, she was met by a "hippie" guy, who never took the other seat next to her. As he approached he looked directly at me. When he reached her he said to her, while looking at me, "Let's move."

For the first time she looked at me, not speaking but looking directly in my eyes. Such a pretty face, but her eyes said it all. Better to have been spit on, then maybe I could have retaliated. But here, all these years later, I still remember the spiteful, hateful look of her eyes.

We went, we served, we did what we were asked.

WILLIAM F. SWEENEY, WORCESTER, MASSACHUSETTS

First, let me state that I served as an infantryman in Vietnam in 1969. Second, let me say that I can accurately recall the mood out on the streets in 1970. It was not pretty.

To ask merely if we were spat upon does us a disservice. It is like surveying assault victims based on whether their left leg was broken. I think that a more accurate service could be rendered by trying to determine how many of us were the objects of direct personal attack—spit, verbal, physical, etc. Then judge the responses.

I wasn't spat upon, but I was called a baby killer by an hysterical female at a party shortly after returning home; I was called a murderer by one of my own relatives. In another incident, I was told by some guy while in the library during graduate school that he didn't want our "fuckin' type" at the school. Dates? First incident April 1971 in Worcester, Massachusetts; second incident July 1971 in Worcester, Massachusetts; third incident November 1975 in New Haven, Connecticut.

Hostility is expressed in many ways. There are many ways to experience rejection. Spit can take many forms. Arriving at the truth is often a fierce and silent battle.

PETER S. TIFFANY, WEST PITTSBURG, CALIFORNIA

When I returned from Vietnam, I was given (received) a message which remains unchanged to this day. I was not to speak of my war experiences to my mother—she could not stand to hear about the realities I had seen, experienced, shared, and lived through. To this day we have not reopened that conversation we had in mid-August 1969, the evening I came back home.

My mother's was simply the first of many similar messages I got within a very short time of my return. Luckily, I got orders for Europe, and I was again among men and women who had served in Vietnam. When we spoke to each other about Vietnam, it was on the side and out of the hearing of those who had not served and survived as we had.

It was not until I returned to the U.S.A. that I again discovered the message was still there. I sought employment in 1973. I was not "spit on" but neither was I hired. Several businesses and industries very quietly let it be known that "druggies" and "baby killers" were unwelcome. On top of that I had a service-connected back disability. The word was out, disabled veterans were looking for a gravy train. Employ one and they would soon have an on-the-job injury which the employer would support for as long as the veteran lived.

Finally in 1976–1977, with the love and understanding support of my wife, I regained confidence in myself and my abilities and I have been working productively since.

My point is being spit on was only one way America and its citizens demonstrated their disagreement with the war and we who did America's bidding for her. The pain and frustration I felt when I finally tried to settle down was extreme. No less or greater than many of my comrades I am sure, but it remains albeit changed. Now I simply find it impossible to place any trust in the political leadership (non-Vietnam veterans) who have the reins of power today.

STEVE R. STINNETT, TRACY, CALIFORNIA

I was aboard the U.S.S. Coral Sea when we returned home in October 1965 after 11 months in Vietnam, being one of the first warships involved in that war. Our home port was San Francisco (Alameda), and when we arrived I remembered our division chief, veteran of World War II and Korea, telling us about the great welcome we would receive from San Francisco as he recalled from experience.

That first day we arrived I had the "duty" so I was not able to leave the ship, but I recall when the chief left and returned about three hours later. He had been punched in the eye; he was a small man, about five feet eight, 155 pounds, early forties, and this caused him to retire since he was wearing contact lenses at the time and he almost lost that particular eye. He told me when he arrived back on board that the world had gone mad and some crazy hippies dressed in weird clothes jumped him, knocked him to the ground, and punched him in the eye. He said there were about 300 of them demonstrating outside the gate, Naval Air Station Alameda, shouting obscenities as the returning veterans waited for taxis to take them to town.

The next day I had liberty but the Navy had buses that day to take us to Oakland. All I saw was about 100 "hippies" outside the gate shouting "baby killers," "baby burners," "get the fuck out of here," etc., etc., as they threw garbage and papers at the bus as we drove by. I made three more tours of Vietnam as a "combat photographer" and that was the only incident I recall during my four years in the Navy from 1964–1968.

At present I am a high school history teacher. This incident is more than 20 years ago, so I am doing my best to try to remember and have the dates and numbers correct. These are the facts, and the chief's name was Burnell. It took me two days to remember his name since I only worked with him on that first tour of Nam for approximately one year.

JOHN T. KRUTELL, YORBA LINDA, CALIFORNIA

After 23 months "in country," I flew into San Francisco in 1967 on a government charter. I did whatever paperwork was required, and caught a flight down to Los Angeles to spend my leave with my parents.

Upon arriving at the Los Angeles airport, I was at the baggage claim waiting for my things to come down on the conveyor. Two kids, teenagers I think, were standing close to me and one commented on the bandages around my neck.

I said I had been hurt in Vietnam and had been released from the hospital to recuperate at home. The second boy allowed as how Vietnam was a bad war, we had no business there, etc., etc., and it was too bad my wound wasn't six or eight inches higher. Or words to that effect.

Being an officer, a gentleman, and a lieutenant of Marines, I turned and walked away, rather than pursue the occasion. But I could have, maybe should have, done other.

I have a sixteen-year-old son who is the most precious person in the world to me. He knows the value of independent thinking and doesn't hesitate to express his views, but he respects the views of others and the right and dignity of individualism. With the events taking place in the Middle East and in South America, I'm scared to death he'll have to go through the horrors I did. My fervent hope is that he won't, but if he does, he'll do his best. And when he comes home, he'll be proud of what he did, as I was. I pray America treats him with the respect and consideration he will have earned.

JAMES F. DAILEY, COLUMBUS, OHIO

I am retired from the United States Air Force, having served in Vietnam and a number of other overseas areas as well.

I was never spit on, but caught hell, more or less, going and coming. In March 1968, I was at Akron/Canton going to Vietnam and caught a bunch of verbal abuse from some young people, not necessarily "hippies" in the true sense of the word. They might have been Kent State students. It bothered me, but I didn't think too much of it at the time.

Coming back in '69, I made it all the way to a United Airlines flight from Chicago's O'Hare Airport to Dayton/Vandalia without incident. On the flight, a businessman—I guess he was a businessman, he had a suit on—didn't like the fact that I was riding in first class. I wanted to get home and it was the only ticket I could get. My appearance may have provoked him. I had a crew cut with white walls and was wearing an Air Force summer uniform that I had worn the night before I left Phan Rang in a bunker. The Army went to Fort Lewis for a new issue, but the Air Force came home in whatever we happened to have on at the time.

The man really chastised me and I had a very difficult time holding my temper, but I wasn't about to get in a fight on-board an aircraft. Besides, I was anxious to get home.

JAMES BENNARDO, HUDSON, MASSACHUSETTS

I served as an air traffic controller with the Navy in the Tonkin Gulf aboard the aircraft carrier Coral Sea in 1969-1970. While in the war zone we provided air support for ground troops and regular bombing strikes in Vietnam, Cambodia, and Laos.

The ship was based in Alameda, California, and would deploy to Vietnam for 10-month stretches. On returning from such cruises, spouses and friends would greet the crew from the Golden Gate Bridge as the ship passed beneath them on its way to the base. The welcome usually consisted of carnations and other flowers dropped from the bridge onto the sailors lined up in formation around the flight deck.

As you can imagine, our return on July 1, 1970, was an unforgettable experience. Though most of us were unaware at the time, the Golden Gate was also a logical spot for protesters. Later reports told of people not only spitting, but urinating (or at least dumping urine) from the bridge onto the ship below. The net effect apparently was flowers, saliva, and urine descending together onto the sailors.

Of course, the height of the Golden Gate Bridge and the strong winds would render such action purely symbolic. We did not feel that direct confrontation. The closest I personally came to such an experience was the occasion when I was verbally abused by a woman in a singles bar for not going to Canada or to jail instead of Southeast Asia.

This brings up another point: Though I agree with the contention that most protesters maligned government leaders rather than the individual servicemen, I must say that I distinctly recall a time when anyone in a military uniform was a potential target for ridicule and abuse. For that reason, I never wore my uniform off the base.

When I found out what some protesters were doing on the Golden Gate bridge as the ships passed beneath—I think my life would have been at least a little bit happier if no one ever thought so lowly of me that he/she would spit or urinate on me. At the very least, ignorance would have been bliss.

I guess it's only fitting that the protest would be somewhat removed and impersonal. The war was that way for some of us: My job as an air controller was distant from combat, and the destruction I contributed to was general, almost abstract—done by remote control, yet still devastating. The pilots I guided, of course, were one giant step closer. I guess we were the lucky ones.

KENNETH E. BAGGETT, HAMMOND, INDIANA

In the Seattle airport, as I was arriving home after serving in Vietnam in 1968-1969, a gang of 10 to 20 total strangers clustered in the terminal and shouted insults at me as I passed by in my uniform.

At the time, I paid them little attention. I was swept up in living, at long last, the dream that had sustained me through the hell of war: I was coming home. I was touching U.S. soil for the first time.

Besides, I simply could not appreciate the magnitude of what they were doing at the time. It never occurred to me that people could be so morally bankrupt that, devoid of any fortitude, they would substitute the safety of one another's company and, together, attack individual young soldiers, who walked through the airport alone in their sacred moment of homecoming.

The longer I was home, however, the more clearly I understood that my Seattle experience was no curious aberration. This was part of an organized effort by a large and vocal segment of our society to ridicule and demean traditional values and strength of character by ridiculing and demeaning those who believed in them.

There is a dangerous myth: That people like my persecutors in Seattle were just as courageous for resisting duty as the men who put their lives on the line. "Bring the boys home?" All I heard was, "Hell, no, we won't go." Why did all this supposedly courageous commitment to peace evaporate once the threat of being drafted was removed? Torture and wholesale massacre in Vietnam and Cambodia increased exponentially when the U.S. pulled out. Why were there no protests then? The answer, of course, is that commitment to peace was never the issue. Resisting service was.

Figuratively, I have been "spat upon" countless times over the years, but not by hippies in airports. I am spat upon every time one of my countrymen prostitutes his values to perpetuate the myth that the easy, comfortable way out of a difficult time for our country was as "courageous" as making hard choices.

I'll suggest a survey. Ask people whether they participated in the airport harassment of returning veterans. Ask them for permission to publish their names and addresses. Let's give them a forum, after all these years of silence, to demonstrate that their courage indeed equals that of the men who laid it on the line in Vietnam.

A brief comment in response to Mr. Baggett's suggestion: When I printed the series of newspaper columns after I first received these letters, I did, indeed, include the invitation for anyone who had spat upon a returning soldier to write in and explain his or her motives, and to reflect on how he or she feels about the subject now.

There were no responses.

BILL CHALMERS, COPPERAS COVE, TEXAS

On the return from my third tour of duty in Vietnam, I had the occasion to experience a distasteful now, humorous then, incident at the airport in San Francisco.

It was in the early morning hours, as I was waiting for the first flight to Dallas. I was wearing a newly issued dress green uniform with ribbons. It was in September 1969.

I was looking at an advertising display for, of all things,

San Francisco baked sourdough bread. A well-dressed young lady walked up to me and asked me in a semi-loud voice, "How many babies have you murdered?"

She seemed to be smiling, and I thought she was putting me on, and I answered, "About 16."

I then realized that she was serious. I was filled with rage and sorrow at the same time. If there had not been a few people in the vicinity, I might have punched her out.

She believed what I told her. I know I have made a terrible mistake and I hope that I have not affected her life as traumatically as she has mine.

FREDERIC R. PAMP, COLORADO SPRINGS, COLORADO

I spent 1969-1970 in Vietnam as a forward observer and fire direction officer with the 198th Light Infantry Brigade, Americal Division. I remember several incidents when I got back to the United States very clearly:

—I ran into a guy who had been a good friend from college and who had been radicalized in the years between our graduation and the next time I saw him (1972) at a party. When he found out where I had been and what I had been doing (by that time I was out of the service and looked like the hippie graduate student I was), he recoiled from me, snarled, called me a murdering bastard, and stomped off.

—I ran into a guy I knew from high school who, when he found out, told me gleefully how he had hired a corrupt doctor to procure a 4-F rating for himself. While this guy was clapping me on the back he allowed as how he was no chump, he had gotten out of it.

—From 1971 to 1974, I was a student at the New York University School of Law. As far as I know, I was the only Vietnam vet in my class and perhaps at the law school. I was generally thought of as an exotic species. Some people were curious, some were repelled. Some refused to have anything to do with me. It was not all bad, of course, and I really think that some women went to bed with me just for the experience of having such a strange and weird person. When Nixon and Kissinger conducted the criminal Christmas bombing campaign and the campuses became unruly, I chose not to boycott class because while I disagreed violently with the bombing, I knew Nixon did not give a damn about boycotts, and when I crossed the picket line I was singled out for abuse.

—I was told by a woman at a cocktail party (circa 1975) that Lieutenant Calley was probably typical of company-grade officers, being brutal and unthinking.

—I was turned down for dates by two girls who had the honesty to tell me they simply could not go out with a killer.

—While in uniform, often at airports (you could fly half fare then, as a standby, if you wore your uniform), I would sometimes run into older men who would tell me they were World War II or Korean War vets, give me the glad hand, and then tell me that most Vietnam vets were druggie bums who were a disgrace to the uniform.

I made a considered decision in 1968, when I enlisted in the Army two weeks before I was to be drafted: Having accepted the benefits this country has to offer, I had a duty to serve, the country had the right to tell me to go in the Army, and the Army had the right to order me to Vietnam. I did and do still think that the war was an awful mistake, that we had no business there, and that we were ruining both their country and ours.

And I did and do still feel that I was given unfair, unreasonable treatment both by some of those who were against the war and some of those who supported it. My point is that some people did not make a distinction between a bad policy and the individuals who had to carry it out.

DONALD S. WATSON, FARMINGTON HILLS, MICHIGAN

I returned to school at Arizona State 20 days after I got back from Vietnam. The reaction to my having been in the service was "exceptionally cool."

Foremost was my experience at the local VFW post. I accepted my three tours in Vietnam as fact and expected that at least members of the same fraternity (foreign-war veterans) would be the most understanding of the people around Tempe, Arizona. Not so, as it turned out.

I joined the VFW only to find that I was not accepted by those other "older" members who had "served with distinction" in Korea or World War II. I visited the post three times, was ignored totally by the membership I met, and was in fact told by one person that Vietnam vets were not welcome.

And so I gradually turned to a segment of the population that accepted me. I grew long hair and protested the war as it grew into a huge obscene case of the U.S. trying to exert its strength against the will of the people of Vietnam.

Interesting, don't you think, that the real acceptance I found was from those younger anti-war protesters who were allegedly spitting on the returning soldiers—while I was ignored by those I had turned to first.

DAVID A. BROWN, WALNUT CREEK, CALIFORNIA

From stories in the Army Times and letters from home I expected a hassle and was prepared to fight anyone who got between me and my flight home to Kansas City. (I returned from Vietnam in January 1970.) In the Denver airport an old veteran bought me a drink when he recognized my unit insignia as that of the unit that had saved his in World War II.

During college we did encounter a lot of resentment but no violent opposition. A girlfriend of the woman I dated did call me the usual names. No one wanted to hear about it, so you let your hair grow long. But you can't hide a twenty-five-year-old freshman in a beat-up field jacket or pea coat. Even most of the vets who were active in campus support groups or political groups wouldn't talk about it. We would talk about R&R and basic training and Europe and buddies—but not about combat and not about killing.

I was luckier in my transition back to the world because I'm from a military family, and stayed on active duty and in the reserves for a while. What was most aggravating was the feeling of being had. One Memorial Day weekend I went to church with my girlfriend in Concordia, Kansas, a typical small farming town; the preacher asked that the veterans stand to be recognized. I was the only one in the place under the age of fifty.

An aside: I am so tired of drug-crazed vet, super-survivalist stories. Most of those guys were fouled up before Vietnam, or would have been anyway. There are a great number of us who are relatively normal.

MAY C. ECKHARDT, STURGIS, MICHIGAN

While my son was home on leave from Vietnam, a Presbyterian minister refused to shake his hand as we were leaving church. He said he could not and would not shake my son's hand because of the killing my son was involved in. Needless to say, my son doesn't venture to church very often even after all these years and different ministers.

LARRY COLEMAN, SAINT ANNE, ILLINOIS

On December 13, 1969, Tacoma, Washington airport, around 9:30 at night, myself with approximately 150 other returning-home Nam vets were being detained in the plane after just arriving 10 minutes before. After another half hour or so we started to get restless and started beating on the windows and emergency exits—you gotta remember, we'd been on an airplane for 18 hours.

Finally the Army or whomever was in charge decided to let us off the plane. While disembarking we were told to wait for the buses which were supposed to be on their way. Yeah, right.

Getting my feet upon home soil again—I remember how clean the air smelled compared to Nam but also how cold it was, it must have been in the low 40s that night and while I was cussing the Army for sending me home in short sleeves I also realized we were out in the middle of nowhere at the far end of the airport. Somebody said the buses were gonna be late so a bunch of us, about 40 or so, started walking toward the biggest building with the most lights on.

After walking and half-running for several minutes we started noticing and hearing a large group of people moving toward us on the other side of a short fence that ran parallel to the direction we were going. To this day I don't know how many there were but we numbered around 40 and I think they outnumbered us about 5 to 1. At first we thought they were our families but we knew better (I believe my own parents thought of Vietnam as a tough summer camp for high school dropouts who probably deserved everything they got anyway).

Somebody said they were the American Legion guys and were probably gonna give us a medal or something, and I remember thinking, Wow, this is just like when ole Frank Sinatra came back after World War II, blue-eyed and handsome and lookin' to get drunk and laid. About this time reality struck me in the shape of a wine bottle three feet in front of me.

It didn't take long for this small-town lad from Kankakee to realize these were real war protesters out there. I mean to tell you, these assholes were really trying to hit us and because we didn't have anything to throw back at them, they really started getting brave and started coming over the fence toward us. The only thing I remember them saying was "Baby Killers, Go Back, Baby Killers, Go Back," over and over, and I started yelling that I didn't kill no fuckin' babies, but if I had a gun I'd waste you motherfuckers.

I didn't know if it was my height or lack of it (I'm five feet four) that prompted one of them to shove her finger in my face or what the reason was, but I'll tell you I just followed that hand up to a face with a right cross. This little ole tunnel rat was pissed. It was about that time I discovered I smashed the face of a girl, and a real tall guy was yelling at me, "Are you proud, killer?" Well I was scared, so I kicked him in the nuts and commenced to beat on his head as he was running back to the crowd.

I'm here to tell you, everybody was hookin' and jabbin', even this old E-9 lifer that sat next to me on the plane. This only lasted a couple of minutes or so and the surviving assholes made it back over the fence. In a matter of seconds flashing lights from every MP and cop car in the state of Washington was there blocking us from having more fun. About this time our buses finally showed up.

To make a long story a little shorter, it wasn't till 13 hours later and several rum and Cokes on the way to O'Hare that the first seed of bitterness started to grow in me. Hey, after almost 20 years I'm still pissed—not at the protesters who were at the airport, they paid the hard way and I doubt if they ever did that again, but pissed at whomever it was that should have kept them out of there. None of us expected a brass band to greet us, but if that many drunk and stoned out of their minds fuckin' hippies could greet us with beer bottles, why couldn't a few patriotic Americans be there with full ones and a couple of handshakes?

That was the last and only time I believe I was ever insulted because of my role as a Nam vet. Please let me take this moment to personally thank everyone who over the past two decades said to me, "Thanks, it must have been hell over there," and all the free beers (probably too many) and also the extra credit I got on my fireman application test from the city of Kankakee for veterans' points. Just the facts, Jack!

SCOTT C. CAMPBELL, LONGMONT, COLORADO

The press had the American people believing so much shit it was unbelieveable—yes, men, women, and children were killed, but what do you do with a 10-year-old kid who leaves a pipe bomb in his bicycle among a group of GIs?

I could go on, but for what reason? The movies "Platoon" and "Full Metal Jacket" have given the American people a glimpse of what really happened over in Nam. Had the people known then what they know now we would have come home to a nation that would hang its head in shame for allowing a mindless government to send its youth to a country where they were not wanted, nor did their shed blood solve anything.

It has taken 10 years for me to lift my head, square my shoulders, and face what I was ordered to do against my will. Mark my words, there will be a day when the American people will call upon the Vietnam vets again. Will they answer?

GARY DAVIS, CHATSWORTH, CALIFORNIA

I am sorry for taking so long to get this in the mail. Since I didn't consider it one of the high points of my life, I guess I've been putting it off.

The time was about March 1969, at Los Angeles International Airport. I was waiting to be picked up by my mother. I was in uniform, which was a requirement to be able to fly "military standby." I was sitting in the waiting area when three guys came up to me. I wouldn't call them "hippies." They had long hair. Well, everyone had longer hair than I did.

They started asking questions about my ribbons. Everything seemed very cordial. They asked if a particular ribbon was for Vietnam. I said it was. They then started chanting "Baby Burner" over and over again. Then they walked off.

Is it hard to believe that someone would not hit them after leaving the jungles? I was just kind of ashamed. I never flew military standby again.

Also—the idea that most of the anti-war demonstrators had a "Send Our Boys Home" theme? I seem to remember a "Hell No, We Won't Go" theme instead. When the draft ceased there was also a sharp drop in anti-war demonstrations.

That's about all I have to say. Actually I have a lot more I could say but it's not what anyone wants to hear. I suppose there is still a lot of bitterness about the whole mess. Seeing people fall all over themselves to get on the "Let's Welcome Our Vietnam Heroes Home" bandwagon is a little hard to swallow.

Patrick W. Gray, Bellevue, Nebraska

When I came back from Vietnam, I was dumb enough to wear my dress uniform in the San Francisco International Airport. This was on April 15, 1970. A nicely dressed woman in her twenties blocked my path and hissed "Goddamned murderer" in my face.

I don't mean to make it sound melodramatic, but I've never forgotten it. And the dozen or so Vietnam veterans I've talked to (I can't talk to World War II vets) all told similar stories.

I guess guys who lose a war get pretty unpopular.

NICHOLAS CHESLEY, SUNNYVALE, CALIFORNIA

I was returning on emergency leave in 1971 to my home state of Wisconsin to attend the funeral of my father. After nine months in combat duty as a door gunner on a helicopter crew I found myself standing in the San Francisco airport waiting for my connection to Chicago and then home to Wisconsin. It was around three in the afternoon and I was tired and haggard from the long flight, not to mention sad and depressed over the death of my father.

I was accosted by four men around the age of twenty. Whether they were hippies or not I can't say. They were dressed in denim bell-bottom trousers and T-shirts. Their hair was very long and two wore beards. It was obvious they had been drinking and two were carrying cans of beer.

They wanted to fight the soldier boy—how brave was I without a gun in my hand? I turned to walk away and they threw beer at me. I continued to walk away and they pursued me through the crowd hollering and yelling obscenities that alluded to my mother, father, and the fact that I was a chickenshit who liked to kill mothers and babies. Thankfully an airport patrolman intervened and I was able to get to my gate to board my airplane.

The second incident occurred during the same trip while I was in the Chicago airport. I went to sit down in the terminal to wait for my flight to Wisconsin. While I occupied the seat a woman in the next seat asked me if I would mind sitting somewhere else. I asked why, thinking I had taken someone's seat. Her reply was that she refused to sit next to a paid killer of women and children. I told her politely that if she didn't want to sit next to me she had better find another seat. This produced a verbal assault that publicly humiliated me to the point that it made me want to crawl under the seat. She eventually left.

The third event occurred not only to me but to several

hundred servicemen and sailors in 1972 when the aircraft carrier U.S.S. Constellation crossed under the Golden Gate Bridge upon return from a tour of duty off the coast of Vietnam. As the ship passed under the bridge, garbage, animal blood, and urine were dumped onto us as part of an organized protest against the war. Although I wasn't hit and couldn't tell if people were actually urinating or if the blood or garbage actually hit the ship, it was the fact that was reported in the news and on the radio that day.

I think that I speak for the majority of the lucky men and women who returned from the Vietnam War. We never expected to return to a hero's welcome nor did we want one. We realized there was a very strong public opinion against the war. However many of us never expected the welcome— or unwelcome—that we did receive.

It's not so much that people spit at us, it's the fact that we were treated with scorn, isolated, and generally were considered to be outcasts of society. We were the ones who were to be blamed for the war. Unpopular war—take it out on the servicemen and women who died, bled, and fought for their countries. I say died because I personally died every day I spent in Vietnam.

All we wanted to do was to get home to our loved ones and re-enter society. Hopefully we would be treated with the dignity of people who had given great personal sacrifice for their country. We weren't.

MIKE CURRAN, CHICAGO, ILLINOIS

I served with the Marines in Vietnam throughout the year of 1969. In May 1970 I returned home for a wedding of my oldest sister. While I was home, friends who were attending Moraine Valley College, in Palos Hills, invited me to a picnic in the forest preserves.

I only knew three of the people in attendance. I discovered

a guy who was there who had been Medevaced from Vietnam because of wounds received from a booby trap. He had been in the Army and was then a civilian with rows of scars all over his body. We spoke of experiences and talked about how nice it was to see American girls once again.

The moment these wonderful American girls (about twenty years of age) at the picnic discovered we were Vietnam vets they treated us with contempt. They called us names and made us the butt of their jokes. Of course we were labeled as warmongers of the worst degree. Ah, it was great to be back in the midst of our fellow citizens.

DENNIS RAMSEY, LONGMONT, COLORADO

Upon my second return from Vietnam, which ended my service time, I wore my greens to Stapleton Airport in Denver. I went to the bathroom to change into my civilian clothes. I started to throw my uniform clothes into a waste can. A shoeshine man asked me what I was doing, and if he could have them. They were his, even down to the shoes.

TOM EYTON-JONES, BENTON, LOUISIANA

I think about the generalized treatment we received. Things such as being charged double for a hamburger, told there are only middle row seats available on an airplane only to board and find the plane half empty when it takes off, having a cabbie reply "So what" when we told him we had just come back from Nam, being ignored by younger siblings' friends, being told your old job isn't available anymore . . . need I go on?

While the American public may have symbolically "spat" upon us, the federal government tried to gobble us up, digest us, and eliminate us as a well-known waste product. We've been fighting ever since to keep the sewers backed up, to prove we won't go away like some bad dream. Movies are a start, the "Welcome Home" idea was good, and the Vietnam Memorial in Washington is something tangible, but I doubt that the government as a whole will ever take the responsibility that it should and say, "We're sorry, we screwed up."

What's being done now will help us live a little better in the future but you can't legislate away memories. What's done is done . . . the mistakes have been made. People are dead, dying, or wishing they were dead. Fortunately, not all of us are in this condition, but we still remember.

GARY C. PETERS, CARLISLE, PENNSYLVANIA

In Vietnam I only tried to do my job and maintain my sanity in a world gone crazy. I served in Vietnam from May 1969 to May 1970 in the 101st Airborne and spent 11 of my 12 months at a small landing zone. I was not a hero. But I also did nothing to shame myself or my country.

When I returned from Nam I was an emotional wreck but I kept it all to myself so my family and friends thought I was okay and acted like I had never left. I entered civilian life with no problems and continued on with my life. But nobody ever gave a damn about what the Vietnam vet had to endure in that war or the emotional scars that never go away.

No, I was never spat upon by a civilian, I was just ignored by a country that didn't care. Then a few years later came the biggest insult to all Vietnam vets. We weren't spat upon by one person, but by the entire country.

I'm referring to the "heroes' welcome" given to the hostages held in Iran. When Iran finally released the hostages the entire country opened up its arms and its heart to their return. I'm sorry for what happened to them but I was very bitter about their reception home and the praise and admiration they received.

I'm fortunate that I returned from Nam alive and was able to handle the emotional pain of spending a year in hell. But many returning vets needed more help, and if the country would have opened its hearts to us, like it did to the Iran hostages, then the pain would have been easier to bear.

A Vietnam vet could take being spat on by one person. What broke our hearts was being spat on by our country.

RAYMOND C. KERNS, AUSTIN, TEXAS

I did not come home expecting a parade down Main Street or anything of the kind, and I did not hang out in bars and brag or complain. I arrived at the air terminal in Toledo about 1:30 a.m. in near-zero weather, still wearing my khakis and GI raincoat. I was met by my wife and two children; we got into our car and drove home. The reception I got from them was all I needed.

But as time went on, I began to FEEL as if someone were spitting on me, figuratively speaking. I was not a typical Vietnam veteran. I had my "baptism of fire" when the Japanese attacked Pearl Harbor in 1941, and I served through that war with minor distinction, having been awarded the Silver Star and the Purple Heart. I arrived home just a month before the war ended, being met in Indianapolis by my wife. We rode home to Ohio on a bus and were met by her parents and her brother—period. No parades, no "hero's welcome"—and I didn't expect one.

And then, after four years as a civilian, I was again back in service for the Korean War. From there, I debarked at Seattle on a pier with a big sign that said something like "WELCOME HOME—AND THANKS FOR A JOB WELL DONE." That was for me and thousands of other veterans returning through that port. Again, except for immediate family, I doubt that anyone really noticed that I'd been away. I didn't expect anything more.

And so, coming home was nothing new to me in 1968. But what was new was all the negative publicity in the media. Vietnam veterans were called the most unpleasant names. It went on and on. It wouldn't have bothered me so much, for I knew my own heart and my own actions and my conscience was clear.

But as the war dragged on and the public attitude became increasingly negative, my daughter also grew older and more aware of the world around her. At the age of twelve, she began to think that the military profession was less than honorable, and this also influenced her younger brother's views as he grew up. Eventually, my morale suffered quite considerably, and the humiliation of being actually spat upon by "hippies" (who, by the way, were usually in groups) would have been a much less painful experience. Things have changed now, but I'll never forget.

JOHN LEARY, BATAVIA, ILLINOIS

Most returning veterans were eighteen to twenty-two years old. At that relatively young age it is almost impossible to express having your feelings hurt and hurt deeply, especially after trying to prove your "manhood" in Vietnam.

In my opinion, most veterans were not even sure what they felt at the time. We returned to political turmoil, peace marches, anti-war and anti-veteran activities . . . and one giant lack of appreciation.

Imagine helping your neighbor move a piano for a full day. When the task is complete the neighbor goes in his house without a word and closes the door. Most veterans moved a piano for over a year (and much worse) and the door was closed on all of us.

I will remember vividly for the rest of my life leaving Vietnam on a plane loaded with Marines. As the plane took off the cheering and tears exploded with the feeling of being off the ground. I remember looking down at the scarred landscape waiting until we got enough altitude to be completely safe. I remember landing in San Francisco and the wild cheering among us in the plane and the feeling of making it home. Then I remember walking by myself through the San Francisco airport to complete indifference. It was then I realized something wasn't right. My loving and close family was elated to have me home, but there was no sense of appreciation from anyone—my friends and people I knew never said anything. No one knew what to say.

The hurt stuck in real deep, and it is hard to think about. It is even harder to think about good young Americans who gave the ultimate sacrifice—they died for their country. Not Hollywood dead, not like in war movies, but dead and gone just like warriors in World War I, World War II, Korea and all the others. All their families got hit with nothing. All the countless others that left chunks of their young and healthy bodies behind returned not as heroes but to a complete lack of appreciation.

I think the turning point was when the hostages came home from Iran. The country went wild and it was great for me to see our country unified and celebrating. But I know, there were not many veterans who didn't envy the hostages and feel despair about their own "return."

I marched in the big veterans' parade in Chicago last summer. I remember the parade just forming up and leaving Navy Pier to start the parade route. One woman was standing alone and clapping her hands and saying, "Welcome home." I cried, it felt so good, even 17 years later. I felt so good to be marching with thousands of Marines who were bursting with pride singing the Marine Corps Hymn. I have always been proud and it was a chance to celebrate that pride. To see people step forward with a picture of their dead son or brother . . . to see disabled veterans step out to shake hands . . . for all of us to wipe a little spit off our hearts.

"To wipe a little spit off our hearts. . . ." It would be
difficult to imagine a more powerful phrase than that one,
and to analyze it too deeply is not appropriate; Mr. Leary
has said it as well as it can be said.

Quickly, though, just the point that what Mr. Leary and so
many others are talking about, clearly, is catharsis. For Mr.
Leary, the catharsis came on the day of the parade. For large
numbers of others, the catharsis comes when they visit the
Vietnam Memorial in Washington. For the thousand-plus
people who wrote to me, there was probably a measure of
catharsis just in the act of writing.

But consider this: For all the veterans who have managed
to find some form of catharsis after these many years, there
are undoubtedly others who yearn to find it—and still can't.
For them, the feelings you have been reading about are still
hidden. If that thought doesn't shake you, you may be un-
shakable.

DANNY KELLY, SANTA CRUZ, CALIFORNIA

Was I spit on at the airport? No. Was I able to find a job
when a prospective employer found out I was a Nam vet?
No. Was I able to get a date with a girl if she knew I was a
Nam vet? No. Was I even welcome at the local American
Legion post as a Nam vet? No. Were my parents able to tell
people without accusations that their son had just returned
from three years in Vietnam? No.

I returned in September 1969 and was in Atlanta, Georgia.
I denied being a vet until recently because I was repeatedly
told that Nam vets had flashbacks and could freak out on the
job. I was repeatedly asked how I could live with myself after

killing all those innocent people. I could have dealt with being spit on by a hippie. I probably would have broken him in two. Being twenty-one and not being able to get a job, a date, a place to live, or a drink with other vets was the hard part. I still remember.

JOE BARTHOLOMEW, CANTON, OHIO

In retrospect, putting aside the issue of the rightness or wrongness of the war or how it was handled, all I know is that when my country asked me for help, I answered the call and to this day, in spite of everything, I'm proud of that. What's sad is that when the smoke cleared and most of us were lucky enough to come home, our calls for help remained unanswered.

Yes, we were spat upon! You want dates, places, and circumstances? For approximately eight years, over thousands of acres in Vietnam, we were spat upon—not with a drop or two of saliva, but rather with millions of gallons of Agent Orange. Yes, we were spat upon by an older gentleman in a red, white, and blue outfit who answers to the name of "Uncle Sam." Thanks to him, his chemical companies, and "Operation Ranchhand," you might say we were spat upon and didn't even know it.

The real issue isn't whether or not we received a ticker tape parade down Fifth Avenue. Personally, my family and friends telling me that it was good to have me home again was all the welcome home I ever needed.

However, I don't think it's unreasonable for us as veterans to want and even expect medical assistance and/or compensation for war-related health problems that have all but devastated whole families.

Yes, we were spat upon—in Vietnam with Agent Orange and again when we came home with Uncle Sam's indifference to our plight.

FERNE BERRY, KEMPNER, TEXAS

During the Vietnam war we were stationed in the Hippie Paradise of northern California. My husband was in the Army for 30 years. Vietnam was his third war so he was pretty well shock proof, but after he returned from a tour there as a combat leader he was in uniform driving a Jeep when he passed a sidewalk full of anti-war hippies. One of them yelled, "Fuck you, Vietnam," and made an obscene gesture. Jim got out of his Jeep and beat him bloody. (My husband was forty-five and crippled up; the hippie was large, young, and healthy.) In this area where we were stationed there were many gathered who were hostile to the Army. But we never let it bother us much.

There are a lot of ways of spitting on people. One of Jim's duties at this time was notifying the next of kin of the death of their loved one. On long trips I went with him. In his best dress uniform he rang doorbells and shattered lives. How he hated it. He seldom had to say anything; they would know why he was there. Most were so decent. They would thank him for coming in person. Both coming and going on these sad trips we passed troops of hippies with their peace symbols whose name for a dead soldier was "fool."

I knew hippies well. Some were likable, most were lazy and good-for-nothing. The anti-war people were nasty. They are probably in Hollywood writing scripts about wild-eyed, profane, violent Vietnam vets. If so, they are in this way "spitting on."

DAVID M. WIESENFELD, JACKSONVILLE, FLORIDA

In 1968 I interrupted my undergraduate education for the purpose of volunteering for the draft. There was an obvious injustice intrinsic to the student deferment. Because of student deferments the war was being fought disproportionately by blacks and poor whites to the virtual exclusion of the middle class. To fight the war with only the non-college segment of the nation's youth was inherently immoral. To take advantage of my own student deferment any longer would have required me to act inconsistently with those beliefs.

It seems obvious that most of my generation did not feel that way. The vast majority of them were quite satisfied to accept deferment (and in some cases to tack deferment onto deferment) in an often strenuous effort to avoid placing themselves on the line for their society. Some even literally abandoned their country by moving to comfortable and convenient Canada. In doing so many of them developed a need to manufacture rationalizations for allowing the non-students of their generation to be drafted (killed or maimed?) in their place. The excuse was that the war was "wrong" or "immoral" and that the "peace" movement was somehow a heroic endeavor.

Upon my return to the university setting after my time in Vietnam, former friends actually told me I was a "fool" to go to Vietnam. Others' reactions implied that I was morally deficient for having volunteered for service—or, perhaps worse, hopelessly out of sync with the conventional wisdom of my generation. Not in style. The absolute last thing I came to expect from my peers was respect for having served. It did not take long to learn to simply be quiet about the fact that I was a Vietnam veteran. The granting of amnesty to draft dodgers who fled to Canada, and their return home after years of "non-suffering martyrdom" could only reinforce the impression that those of us who served in Vietnam were indeed fools.

If the time ever comes that there is a general agreement that the draft dodgers are the heroes and the soldiers are the fools, there will no longer be an Army and probably no longer a country worth defending.

SAM MAGGIO, WHEATON, ILLINOIS

I came back on a stretcher in a military plane with a bunch of tubes sticking out of me. I'd been in Vietnam over five months and spent two weeks in an Army hospital in Japan. The soldier cringes in shame that he stands up in battle, gets shot at, gets wounded, and his own country hates him. How did this happen?

When I got back I called my girlfriend on a Saturday night and she wasn't home. She had her own apartment and she was out basking in her newfound sexual freedom. I saw her a few weeks later, and Harry Chapin said it best: "Whatever we had once was gone." She thought she had it rough while I was gone.

I met a girl in Kansas a week later and even though I had a cast on my leg and big red scars all over my body she had trouble believing that I was just a month out of the jungle. I ended up seeing her for three or four years and I loved her a lot. She was too nice a girl and I was messed up at the time. I blew her off for her own good just like I did with other women later.

Another girl in Colorado—the same thing. I had a short but loving relationship with an Air Force girl. I'm pretty sure I fathered a child with her but I'll never know for sure. The child would be almost eighteen now. I would have done right by her but she got shipped to the Orient and I never saw her again. She never contacted me. I've spent maybe 4,000 hours since then thinking about it.

When I got out it took a few months for my hair to grow out so I could pass for normal. I couldn't get a regular date if the girl knew I was in the war. If you mentioned Nam they had to go or they changed the subject. None would acknowledge your pain or your experience. You just kept it inside. It wasn't wise to put down that you had been in Nam when you filled out a job application, because they'd think you would bring your problems to work—if you showed up at all.

I sat on all of these feelings for 19 years, and now it is good to get it off my chest. We grew up on John Wayne movies. We were ripe for the picking when the war came. They told us that if we didn't stop the Commies in Nam, we would "see the Commies come marching down our streets." So we ended up saps for LBJ.

The people who turned their backs on us might not be able to find a soldier when they need one next time. Almost every male in my family has been in the military, but it ended with me. They'll have to kill me to get at my son.

DAVE LOGAN, NEW MARSHFIELD, OHIO

Three months ago I was transferred to a new department here at work. I told my boss I was a Vietnam veteran. He says, "Gee, I never would have guessed. You look and act so normal."

Guess that was just a mild spray.

BOB MOON, BURLINGAME, CALIFORNIA

When I returned home from Vietnam in 1968 and again in 1969 I wasn't met at the airport by long-haired anti-war protesters wanting to spit on me; I was greeted by friends and family who treated me with an attitude of indifference that bordered on insouciance.

I was a curiosity. I had learned to deal with life (and death) with an emotional detachment that frightened those who asked the inevitable question: "How many people did you kill?" Not enough. Too many. No answer I could give them would satisfy them, or me.

I learned quickly to keep quiet about my Vietnam service when I saw what Hollywood was doing to the story . . .

drug-crazed baby killers. The war was lost. I was a loser. It's only a movie.

I went back to college on the G.I. Bill and was resented by my peers for the free ride. I sought dental care from a doctor who charged me and the V.A., and that was a no-no, but he still complained when I asked for my money back. With my degree in hand and a heart full of hope I tried to go on to graduate school, but the war was newly lost and I was an embarrassment. . . . Vietnam was not where it's at. It's weird. When I was in college in the early Seventies I was privileged because I was a single, young, white male and therefore could not take advantage of any special grants, programs, etc. Now that I'm out of school, I'm a minority, I'm considered underprivileged because I'm a vet. I'm still me— who are they?

The Wall. Designed by an Asian-American woman no less. Black granite etched with the names. There it is. A beginning. An end. Stand there in front of his name, look carefully at your fully erect reflection, and tell yourself how much you've suffered, how much you've lost. Try to lie to him, to yourself. Never happen.

Back home with a renewed sense of purpose. Told yourself the next few years were going to be rough, and they were. Drying out, just me and I don't like what I see. So what's all this I've been hearing about post-traumatic stress syndrome? Me angry? Me frustrated? Sure I have a gun but it's only for self-defense. Yeah, just like your buddy Mike who self-defensed himself right out of this world. Get a grip. Get in a group. Get in touch with who you were, who you are, and where you're going. You got two trails to choose from; you do have a choice.

Spitting on soldiers? Myth or reality? Perhaps one vet will relate a true story of being confronted by protesters and being spat upon. Or maybe it's just another "urban legend."

Who needs myths when there's enough reality to go around for everybody?

Sorry for the strident tone of this.

DONALD W. WRIGHT, KILLEEN, TEXAS

I was a Marine who served three tours in Vietnam. On my second return—in March 1968—fresh from combat in Hue City, my plane landed in San Francisco, and several of my buddies and myself had to report into Treasure Island Marine Depot, so we hopped a bus into San Francisco.

It was around 2 a.m. when we arrived at the bus station. We got off the bus to check out the town. Within a few minutes the three of us saw a group of young females coming toward us. One of us said, "Good evening."

Another of us said, "What are you all up to?"

In answer, one of the females called us "mercenaries," another called us "baby killers," and one—this one really hit home—called us "paid assassins." There were other things said, but these three I remember.

The first American women we had seen in a long time— hello, welcome home, here's what you get. We did take it and did nothing—we were speechless and basically unable to react. Guys who were alive because of fast reflexes and minds were stopped dead not by bullets or bombs, but by words from our own people.

JOYCE C. NICODIN, COLORADO SPRINGS, COLORADO

My husband is a Marine combat veteran of the Vietnam War, serving there in 1968. He is not writing this because he says it doesn't matter, and besides he wasn't spat on by hippies in the airport, so why hear from him? Maybe he's right.

But there is more than one way to be spat on, and by the attitude and behavior of the American people, my husband

was spat on over and over again. He did show up at an airport
in full uniform. Just his dad met him there, his mother and
sister didn't bother to come along. Then his dad tells him he
should never have gone. That he was stupid to have gone.
Questions like, ''Were you part of those who burned, raped,
and pillaged for our government?''

There is a healing in America of the psychological wounds
of Vietnam, and that's fine. The tangible evidence of this
healing makes most people feel good. But patriotism today
is a fad, costing nothing. It's easy to be patriotic, and desirable. Patriotism in 1968 cost arms, legs, eyes, and life. Patriotism in 1968 cost acceptance by the nation.

My husband says the inner healing of the combat veteran
started a long time ago, by necessity. Those who could, adjusted to their undesirable status in America; those who
couldn't, killed themselves, have gone crazy, or escape
through drugs and/or alcohol. My husband feels the combat
veteran, the one who was right there on the front, fighting
and sweating it out, for the most part still feels the betrayal
of the American people. We weren't there when they needed
us.

WILLARD RICHARDSON, ATWOOD, TENNESSEE

On the front end, I never expected to be welcomed home
by bands and parades. I was drafted into the Army in January
1966 and was in Vietnam by September 1966 for a tour of 12
months. I was sent there by the people of this country; maybe
not directly, but indirectly by their choice of this country's
lawmakers.

Those same lawmakers have a promise to keep—to care
for those veterans who return from war, never to be the same
again, whether disabled from wounds or disease. I was twenty
years old at the time and accepted my fate—to do my duty
to serve my country.

When my fellow soldiers and I left Vietnam (100th Engineers Floatbridge Company), we spent the entire night at the deportation center partying and never slept on the following 15-hour flight back to the States. The anticipation and elation of going home, alive and well, was so great; there are no words to express that wonderful feeling. As for a parade and welcome home, I was not looking for one. To get home as quickly as possible, without interruption, was my only concern.

I had to go on a dialysis machine (13 years) as the result of a kidney disease caused by my service in Vietnam. In 1981 I was elected mayor of my town. As a disabled Vietnam veteran, I give my town all my time and my best for $12.50 per month.

HIRAM G. CRUISE, SAN PABLO, CALIFORNIA

I was eighteen years old at the time I was sent to Vietnam. I was a L.U.R.P., which is a recon specialist. When I returned home no one spit on me. As a matter of fact until the trial of Lieutenant William Calley I was totally ignored.

Then a rash of Vietnam movies, random violence by some vets, and public condemnation. People who knew nothing of me, nor my role in the conflict, called me a baby killer. Employment became difficult as I was flat out asked if I suffered from some sort of mental trauma from the experience. Prime among their concern was drug use. Many times I was asked if I was a crazed druggie.

Services were cut for "He who bore the battle, his wife and dependents"—a Veterans Administration credo. Many of my friends have children with birth defects due to Agent Orange. Psychological problems, and a sense of guilt are just now cropping up in a large number of men.

I am now forty-two years old, married for twenty years to my wonderful wife. My daughter is an honor student in college who will attend medical school. My son is a sophomore in high school and doing well. We own our own home. I have two dogs and my health is fairly good.

No, no one spit on me then, nor would they as I am a large person! I was helped by these "longhairs," as without the pressure put on our government to stop a totally senseless war we might still be fighting. I was spit on by a society so numbed into complacency that were Vietnam just starting right now, no one would murmur a whisper. Except those 2 million vets who would be the "hippies" this time by their disapproval of our involvement in such a war.

*"I Would Like
to Tell Another Side
of the Story . . ."*

*There were letters that did not fit into any of the categories
you have already read about. Some were from veterans; some
were from relatives of veterans; some were from people who
never served; some were from people who just felt compelled
to have their say.*

*Originally I had intended not to include these letters. But
upon reflection, perhaps they are the most appropriate way
to end this book.*

DANIEL G. MCCOY, SACRAMENTO, CALIFORNIA

You cannot imagine how the return to the United States—
"the World," in Vietnam parlance—gets built up in a soldier's mind during his months overseas. Every veteran with
whom I have spoken remembers the exhilaration when the
"Freedom Bird" lifted off the runway to begin the flight
back to "the World."

I had just completed a 22-hour plane ride, 18 hours of
discharge processing, and had been dumped at the San Fran-

cisco airport when I was hissed at and verbally harangued by some civilian travelers . . . made to feel like a misfit in the country I had gone to Vietnam to protect.

There should be no presumption that all Vietnam vets were ready to hurt someone in response to the disrespect of a civilian. In fact, most veterans were trying to do everything they could do NOT to call attention to themselves, and to sublimate the military training they received. Remember, the anti-war feeling in the U.S. by the late '60s/early '70s was great. You might ask, well, what were the returning soldiers doing walking around in their uniforms? Please understand that most Vietnam vets, like myself, were draftees. We were prohibited from owning civilian clothes while overseas, and most were inclined to go home upon release rather than to a clothing store. We were issued fresh dress uniforms upon release which were worn on the trip home. Though I still have that uniform, I have never worn it since.

No matter what section of this book you turn to, you will find references to the uniform. For Mr. McCoy, it is a question of never having worn it since coming home. For others, there was an obsession to take it off just as soon as the plane touched down at an American airport— even to the extent of going into a public restroom, stripping off the uniform, and throwing it away. For others, there is the regret that they were unable to wear it because of the reaction it would engender in civilians. And for still others, there was a desire—a mixture of pride and defiance—to flaunt it and wear it no matter what anyone else thought.

Uniforms are deeply symbolic; that's their purpose. But in the context of Vietnam—and in the context of the stories you have been reading here—the uniforms from that war seem to carry a symbolism that is particularly strong and lasting.

THOMAS H. JENKINS, JR., UNIVERSAL CITY, TEXAS

I am a retired Air Force officer. In 1967 or 1968, while I was stationed in Washington, D.C., I was summoned to a hastily called meeting at the State Department. I was in uniform (optional at that time) and caught a D.C. bus.

One stop before my stop, a very stout lady—I would say 225 to 250 pounds—struggled out of her seat and by the time she pulled the cord the bus driver had passed her stop. She moved up the aisle, planted herself in front of the middle exit door, and proceeded to berate and curse the driver for missing her stop.

I then pulled the cord for my stop. The bus stopped. I said to the lady, "Excuse me, I need to get off." I couldn't get around her.

She stopped cursing the driver, who was preparing to move out. She turned to me and said, "Why in the fuck aren't you in Vietnam?"

I had only recently returned from Vietnam, coincidentally. I will not bore you with some of the retorts that crossed my mind. In all honesty—being in uniform, an officer, and a Virginian—I merely repeated, "Excuse me," and found a way around the obstacle.

Incidentally, I made my meeting on time. In retrospect, I find the incident amusing.

MEGAN MEADOWS, SAN MATEO, CALIFORNIA

My brother did two tours in Vietnam. During that time I remember him coming home twice. The first return visit home was in his uniform, looking and feeling mighty proud to be doing a good deed for our country.

The second time he came home to stay. When I saw him, he was in civilian clothes—I remember a striped T-shirt and beige corduroy pants and brown boots.

I guess sometime later I must have asked him why he didn't wear his Air Force uniform home. I distinctly remember him saying that if he had worn it, he would have been spat on by the people at the airport who were against the war and who didn't understand that he was over there fighting for them. He said that the people were his own age—people he went to school with.

I must have been all of twelve years old at that time, but I will never forget the emptiness and sadness in my big brother's eyes. He was my hero.

STANDLEY H. DAVIS, LA VERNIA, TEXAS

My story is a little different. At the end of June 1969 I was a returning Vietnam vet—a thirty-year-old captain finishing a year as a communications officer in the First Cavalry Division.

My next assignment was in New Jersey. Airline tickets were discounted to military personnel in uniform, so I was flying from San Francisco to Philadelphia in uniform.

My assigned seat was next to a pretty young woman about twenty years old, who was very well dressed and seemed "prim and proper." After takeoff she went to the lavatory and returned wearing a baggy plaid shirt, bib overalls, and sandals, with her hair in one big pigtail, and carrying a tote bag. I was very surprised, and a little apprehensive about what I was in for during the five-hour trip.

She turned out to be very nice, well-spoken and conversational—not at all fitting my stereotype of a "hippie." We made pleasant talk about her school and my wife and children. She didn't ask any questions about Vietnam or make any snide comments or accusations.

Upon landing in Philadelphia I went to the baggage claim area. While waiting there, just standing around, out of the corner of my eye I caught some quick movement. As I turned toward it, the girl from the plane ran up, kissed me on the cheek, and ran away. I was so surprised that my mouth just fell open. As I rubbed my cheek I looked around and noticed several people watching me—and her—and smiling. Then I smiled, too.

Now . . . a change of subject, if you don't mind.

After my retirement from the Army in 1978, I joined the VFW, the American Legion, and the Military Order of the Purple Heart. None of these organizations met my needs nor made me comfortable. I've dropped out of all of them.

I have watched, with great interest, the news coverage of Vietnam vet activities, such as parades, monument dedications, and protests. I even participated in the unveiling and dedication of the San Antonio Vietnam Veterans Memorial.

The feelings I get about the memorials, and the belated recognition and appreciation, are very emotional. I'm thankful for all of it. But I'm ashamed, chagrined, embarrassed, and mortified by the activities of many of the so-called veterans of the Vietnam War—at least the ones we see and hear so much on the news. I suspect a lot of them are phonies. Most of those who claim to be unable to find work are just too weird-looking for the employers. They are more "hippie" than the ones they complain about.

I also have very strong feelings and opinions about the way that the U.S. military and the Vietnamese were sold out.

The blame doesn't go alone to the press, to the public, or to the government. Each contributed in large measure and each was influenced by the others.

Regardless, the "chicken or egg" situation resulted in the loss of the war. But the real loss was far, far greater. This great nation lost face in the world, lost the respect of allies and adversaries, and most of all, we Americans lost our self-respect and our mutual respect.

The strongest opinion I have is this, though. The U.S. may have lost the Vietnam War, but the U.S. military DID NOT lose it! We were not allowed to win it.

PETE ZASTROW, CHICAGO, ILLINOIS

I am a coordinator for Vietnam Veterans Against the War. As an organization of Vietnam vet-peaceniks (how dated that sounds), we were on both sides of the supposed conflict between returning soldiers and anti-war protesters. The "spit-upon-veteran" is a myth we have been attempting to deal with since the war ended.

In the late '60s and early '70s, we believed—and still do believe—that the fiction of the hippie spitting on the deplaning veteran was propagated (at least in part) by those who wanted to make sure that the natural alliance of veterans and peace forces would never take place. The longer it took for the veterans of Vietnam and the protesters of our involvement in Vietnam to join, the better it was for Johnson/Nixon—and for the politicians of today who would hope to be able to repeat a Vietnam-style war in Central America.

When I came home, even though (or perhaps because) I thought I had wasted a year in Vietnam and had no wish to support the military presence, I would have tried to chew off the throat of a spitter. Though I knew I had been wrong in Vietnam, I still believed in the rightness of "serving my country." I had just come back from a year of act first, think later; my reaction would have been violent—and I think that would have been common. On a more practical level, at least 98 percent of troops returning from Vietnam landed at U.S. bases (Travis Air Force Base in California being one of the largest)—no spitters allowed.

But the story persists. Everytime we have heard it—and that must number in the hundreds by now—and have been in a situation to talk to the storyteller, we have discovered (after sometimes many questions and attempts to pin down facts and times, etc.) that he is telling a story he "heard" from someone. In rare instances we have found people who firmly believe their story about being spit on is true, but the facts surrounding the story make it impossible. Unfortunately, they have told the story so many times it has become a part of their being (which is, after all, what a myth is) and they cannot give it up just because they are confronted with fact.

Vietnam Veterans Against the War was not welcomed by the peace movement with fervor back in the early days; there was suspicion of those who had been off killing Vietnamese even if we were ordered to do so. The understanding that there was an important distinction between the warrior and the war—that came later and was not an easy battle for Vietnam vets to win.

But I would be much surprised to find that the spitting had really happened even once.

BIFF MORSE, WINFIELD, ILLINOIS

I served with the Fifth Infantry Division from July 1968 to July 1969. I didn't use drugs in Vietnam, but I drank heavily. I had D.T.'s on the way home and landed in an Ohio mental health center. The first thing the admitting doctor asked was, "What drug did you take on the plane?"

I was never told I had the D.T.'s. I thought it was an

emotional breakdown. I figured out it was the D.T.'s about two years later.

While home on leave that August, none of my family or friends wanted to hear about the war. They thought I should try to forget. At parties, people would tell me that talk of the war was a bummer, so why didn't I just relax and have fun?

I served another year and a half in the Army—six months in Washington, D.C. We wore our dress greens to work and endured many dirty looks. People in my age group would smile and be friendly only when they learned I had come to oppose the war. People on the other side of the generation gap would smile and be friendly only until they learned I had come to oppose the war.

I felt the only value anyone placed on my opinion was if they could use it to reinforce their own. Otherwise, my experience (and my life) was inconsequential.

KATHY PARKHOUSE, COLORADO SPRINGS, COLORADO

As the wife of a Vietnam veteran, I would like to tell another side of the story. I went to college in the Sixties and participated in anti-war rallies. I became convinced that anyone who voluntarily went to Vietnam was at best weak-willed, and at worst a "fighting man" who thought nothing of killing others.

It was not until I started working at an Army hospital in 1971 that my attitude underwent a 360-degree shift. There I talked to many veterans and discovered that many of them grappled with the incongruity of what they were doing; that many were proud of their tour of duty; and that many felt Vietnam was "all in a day's work."

In 1973 I met my future husband and learned firsthand what it was like "over there." On our first date, we went to an ice cream parlor. When the siren went off because someone had ordered a large soda, my husband dived under the table. I still only have glimpses of what it must have been like for him—he won't talk about it.

I still have many conflicting feelings about Vietnam—I am trying to work them out, but I am not sure I will ever be able to completely. I have wanted to make an apology for a long time for my naive and oversimplistic views. War is never an easy issue to resolve in one's mind, and I do apologize to all of the soldiers for assuming that theirs was an easy task.

In case you are wondering—no, I never spit on a veteran, and such an idea was and is repellent to me.

JOSEPHINE TALTY, DENVER, COLORADO

I write this with sadness and caring. I am the mother of two Vietnam vets. One returned and one didn't. The one who didn't was my youngest son, just twenty-two. He wasn't drafted—he enlisted "because the world needs to be a better place and I promised Walter if anything happened to him I would fill his place." Walter, his best friend, was killed in Vietnam at seventeen years of age.

I know the outrage these men feel because I, too, was questioned about my sons being in an "unjust war"—once the day he was buried, and other times smugly by parents whose boys avoided the call of their country.

LOUISE BIELFELT, SONOMA, CALIFORNIA

I did not spit, but I do remember the time of 1970-1971 and the war. I had two small sons, ages 7 and 5. Every week we made cookies and delivered them to the Oakland U.S.O. At Christmastime I served "ditty bags" for the Red Cross, and the boys and I shopped for toilet articles and gifts. We wrapped them all and filled our bags. One Christmas we invited two soldiers to spend the day with our family, then have Christmas dinner. It wasn't much, but we tried to help.

Sorry it is only the bad moments that get remembered so often.

PEGGIE KNOBLES, STOCKDALE, TEXAS

Our Jimmy was not spit on—he was killed. He was an air observer with the Fourth Battalion, 42nd Field Artillery. He was the liaison officer for Charlie Battery located at Fire Base Winnie approximately 10 miles southeast of An Khe. On September 11, 1970, he was conducting a mission of visual reconnaissance when the observation helicopter he was on went down. He was twenty-five years old. He left a wife and baby daughter, three brothers and a sister, myself, and his father. Jimmy was our first-born, the big brother the rest of the children looked up to. The husband who wasn't coming home, the father who his daughter would never know.

Because it was an unpopular war many chose to forget those killed and wounded were fighting in the service of their country. Draft dodgers who deserted their country received a warmer welcome home from their tour of Canada. At the City Hall of our little town there stands a Memorial for the boys who died in World War I and World War II. Nothing for the two boys who were killed in Vietnam. No, Jimmy was not spit on, but just killed. And forgotten except for those that loved him.

What is "to spit"? Look in the New World Dictionary. Spit—to eject from within the mouth; to utter explosively (to spit out an oath); to express contempt or hatred.

I would like to particularly tell you about another Vietnam veteran. He came to work as a lab and X-ray technician for the same group of physicians that I worked for. He had served two tours in Vietnam and was retired from the Army. But "Hondo" was different—he wore faded jeans and a long beard, skinny as a rail and had a "I don't give a care" attitude.

He was immediately dubbed an upstart—he was that man in the lab with the beard. He was shunned by the townspeople. He was an outcast. But let me tell you, the real losers were the ones who did not take the time to know Hondo. This happened in 1978-1980 in Floresville, Texas. No one will ever know how I miss that kind and gentle soul. Hondo died in 1983 from too much radiation while a medic in Vietnam. I went to Hondo's funeral—I was the only one there from our county. His family put him to rest at Fort Sam Houston.

No, I did not see any spit coming from anyone's mouths. Only from their hearts.

REVEREND PAULA MAEDER CONNOR, BEXLEY, OHIO

Having been on what some folks call the "other side" of that time as a Peace Corps volunteer in Thailand, I have a different view. I was a teacher of secondary English in Chantaburi, Thailand, with the U.S. Peace Corps from 1972-1974. Chantaburi is located about a five-hour bus ride southeast of Bangkok on the Gulf of Siam. Between Bangkok and Chantaburi were located two U.S. military installations. One was Sattahip . . . a deep water port dug with (as I understand) U.S. Navy assistance. The other was Utapao . . . a U.S. air base with visible airfields from the road upon which I traveled Thai bus transit from Chantaburi to Bangkok and the return about once a month.

Each time I passed I would count the tails of the B-52's that sat on the airfield. Some days I would count as many as 40 before the bus had moved on and I could count no more. Other days I remember less . . . many less. It is an awesome sight . . . these big machines one after the other after the other . . . like a huge graveyard of black stones in finned trapezoidal shape.

My first year in Chantaburi I remember much disdain for

those big death machines. I remember thoughts of how awful the military folks must be to be there. I remember years of membership in the Air Force ROTC auxiliary, Angel Flight, at Capital University in Bexley, just a few years prior to this Peace Corps stint. I remember how I felt as if light years had passed between Angel Flight (1967-1969) and the Peace Corps. I wondered what caused my ''conversion'' and what kept others in a different era.

The hotel in Bangkok nearest the Peace Corps office (I simply cannot remember its name) was also the Bangkok R&R hotel for the Green Berets. I remember sitting in its small restaurant and getting glares, stares, and swears from some Green Berets who had been in the forests and jungles of northeast Thailand and beyond for months and who were now on leave—in a foreign land with foreign women— looking at white round-eyed women who (at least on my part) were scared of these military guys. I remember rude invitations for sleeping with them. I remember cold shivers after seeing accommodations for prostitutes . . . complete with chairs about hip level which included stirrups. I remember wondering and feeling equally far away from home, family, innocence. I remember growing into the reality of a wonderful Asian culture affected in many ways by U.S. presence. I remember.

The second year I was in Thailand I ''came around'' a bit and happened upon an American missionary to U.S. military personnel at Utapao. I had numerous occasions to visit this place called ''The Vine'' and to meet some airmen. In visiting the area outside the base itself I also had the opportunity to see the low-rent housing for GI's and the rented wives and the beautiful bi-racial children . . . Amer-asian and Afroasian . . . lovely, exquisite human beings . . . hated by their own society for being of mixed race. They ran in the streets and played all the children's games with their neighbors. I wonder today how those now-young adults are, where they are, if they are.

In meeting some of the airmen I came to realize that they didn't really want to be loading bombers . . . but it was their job. I came to hear the pain of their profession and the eeriness of loading a B-52 only to reload it the next day or so. I saw their tears.

Last year one of my Thai former students called me. He came and stayed a week at our home and shared stories of life for him over the past years. He is a medical doctor by profession, yet little money is to be had. He has chosen to pay off the government in Thailand and be done with his debt to them. He has taken up a lucrative business enterprise. My former student was tops in his class and a scholar at one of Thailand's best universities. I taught him English in the equivalent of seventh and eighth grades so that when he got to college he could study in English as most Thais did then. He is, as many young people here in the U.S., into "success-ism" and the chase for the big bucks.

I never spit on a GI. I cried with them and for them. I mourned their presence in a beautiful land. After being with my former student I wonder if my presence there ought also be mourned.

Between 1974 and now I have been to the seminary, been pastor of a small country church, done postgraduate work in feminist and pastoral theology, become a university pastor, posed and listened to a million questions about the meaning of life, and grown light years . . . perhaps, perhaps.

Light years . . . perhaps.

DALE WHITE, CANTON, MICHIGAN

My tour of duty in Vietnam was from December 1966 to September 1970. I left for Vietnam, as many did, an eighteen-year-old with stars in his eyes and visions of glory.

Like most I was scared yet proud. I was also considerably more naive than most.

During my first year in Vietnam I heard rumors about the protesters Stateside. After awhile my family even started to mention them in their letters to me. I thought we were conducting ourselves in a humane fashion in Vietnam. We were, after all, running medical facilities, rebuilding hamlets and villages, helping the orphanages, and building roads and bridges. So we paid little attention to the protest movement—figuring, I suppose, that it would die a quiet death.

On my first furlough Stateside I ran into a vague acquaintance from high school. He had a thousand questions, most of them anticipated and normal: "How bad is it over there? Have you seen a lot of action? Is it as hot as they say?" Then he followed with the zinger: "Have you had to kill any women or kids? We've heard how whole villages are being wiped out." It so shocked and astounded me I couldn't answer. To think that normal people could actually believe that garbage.

I NEVER saw any of our people commit any of the atrocities as trumpeted by the media and the protesters of that era. Oh, yes, there were a great many barbarous atrocities committed. These atrocities were suffered by our own wounded, dead, and POWs. They were suffered by civilians who did nothing more than accept needed aid from us. More than once I watched hardened combat vets puke their guts out after viewing the enemy's handiwork. I include myself among those combat vets.

The following year I flew back for another 30-day furlough with another vet. We stopped at a diner on Plymouth Road in Livonia for a real American hamburger and milkshake—our way of convincing ourselves we were really home. We were approached by the first hippie either John or I had ever seen. This fellow then proceeded at the top of his lungs and with much profanity to tell us and anyone else within earshot that we were murderers, invaders in a country that didn't want us, and that if we had any guts we should desert and go to Canada. It was at this point that John and I offered to pool our money, drive him to Metro airport, and buy him a one-way ticket to Hanoi so he could fight with his friends. He beat a retreat from the diner screaming obscenities over his shoulder. Unfortunately we would hear variations of that theme for the remainder of our leave.

In 1969, while on medical leave from Vietnam, I took my mother up the road to have lunch and to get reacquainted. When we got up to pay and leave the fellow in the next booth got up and blocked our path. This was not a hippie or some punk protester—this was a man in his thirties, blue-collar worker, probably married and with one or two kids of his own. He insisted on informing me that I wasn't a real soldier and I didn't know what war was because he had fought in Korea! He said anyone could get a Purple Heart now just for the asking, and that the three I now wore were bullshit. This man, supposedly the mainstay of our country, was prepared to start a fight at 2 o'clock in the afternoon in a restaurant. Who the hell was this guy? I didn't know him, had never met him, nor done anything to him. Was the whole country being brainwashed?

It was then and is now beyond my power to describe the anger and hatred I felt then, and still feel today. What intelligent people we have bred that they can be led by the nose by whoever makes the most noise!

As disappointing as I'm sure it must be to some, I am not some neurotic vet desecrating society every time I'm released from the psych ward of the local VA. In fact I'm married with three kids (none of them neurotic either), a $100,000 home in the suburbs, and my own company.

My feelings are still strong and buried just slightly below the surface. Today I do business with a great many of these same people who symbolically, if not physically, spit on us when we came home from Vietnam. They think I'm a great guy. I don't boast about my service time, yet I don't hide it, either. I wait with patience hoping that some day these very same people will have the opportunity to burn in hell while I laugh.

ANDREA DENSLEY, NORTH LAS VEGAS, NEVADA

In 1965 I was 10 years old. My fifth grade teacher, an insightful woman, assigned the class members to each write to a serviceman. I chose to write to the father of a friend of mine. As a child, his reply moved me, and I've kept his letter all this time.

He wrote from Bien Hoa, Vietnam, November 15, 1965:

". . . It is a wonderful feeling to know that there are those people in the world who love us enough to write of their appreciation . . . Communism seems to know no bounds and the people who embrace it continually strive to force that way of life on the free peoples of the earth. It is a big job to deter their efforts. This is our job here . . . My heart fills with pride to know that I am an American . . . (Signed, Ray A. Young, Captain, United States Army)."

I grew up, the war escalated. The fear that my big brother might be drafted tugged at my heart. To be honest, I had no opinion of the war or its morality. Yet I was so proud, and in awe of, those young people who went—those who didn't burn their draft cards or flee to Canada. They were AMERICANS.

The side of the "wounded" veterans, and the side of the anti-war protesters, are frequently examined. The "third side" of the story is those of us who, perhaps as I, were too young or politically ignorant to vocalize their feelings.

I had a friend in college who had been a helicopter pilot in Vietnam. I tried on a few occasions to talk with him about it. I wanted to understand, to express my appreciation, to sympathize in my meager way with the horrendous experience it had been for him. He always deftly changed the subject, and I let it go. The experience is similar to empathizing with someone whose closest family member has died. You never know what to say, so, often you say nothing.

I know I can't be alone in these feelings. It is monstrously asinine to blame the Vietnam veterans for the war. The majority of them may not even have supported it. Yet to me an important fact is those veterans loved America enough to sacrifice their lives, their sanity, their selves, regardless of their political leanings. I deeply apologize for my silence.

KAY SCHWARTZ, ADDISON, ILLINOIS

In the 1960s my husband and I were in our twenties and raising three little boys.

The drug culture was in and soldiers were not the only ones being spat upon. We were working hard trying to raise our children and teach them what we considered the real values of life. The media, college professors, students, authors, movie makers, etc., were all telling us that our values were pure manure.

We were told that drugs were fine—they didn't do anyone or society any harm. We were told that we were materialistic asses because we wanted a nice home for ourselves and our children. We were told we were immoral because we believed in democracy and this country. It was like being bombarded all day every day with utter disrespect for all we were trying to live and teach our children to value.

Every night there was the war in Vietnam in our living rooms. War was no longer just for soldiers—it was there in color and all its horrors every day on the TV with our children asking over and over, why were our soldiers doing that? And the media telling us over and over that our boys were on dope, were murderers and fools for being soldiers. We couldn't answer any of the questions for ourselves or our children.

So we shut it off and shut it out. My husband and I love to read. We read everything we can get our hands on, but for the 10 years after the Vietnam War we read nothing about the war. It took us 10 years to be able to start to read again about that period, and to be able to discuss it.

On the 10th anniversary of the end of the war, my son made me up a banner on the computer, which we put across the front of the garage. The banner said: "Vietnam—10 Years—We Remember. To Those Who Died—Thank You. To Those Who Returned—Welcome Home."

We put the banner up at 6 in the morning before my son left for college. At 7 in the morning I was sitting on the front porch having coffee and a young man came by delivering telephone books. He went up to the garage and read the banner. He came over to my porch and put the telephone books down, and stood there crying.

He said, "Lady, I love your sign."

I started crying and said, "I'm sorry it's 10 years late."

We were both crying, and then he said, "Lady, it is never too late."

He left still crying and I sat there crying for all of us.

About the Author

BOB GREENE IS A SYNDICATED COLUMNIST FOR THE *Chicago Tribune*. His column appears in more than two hundred newspapers in the United States. He is a contributing editor of *Esquire*, where his "American Beat" column appears each month, he is a contributing correspondent for "ABC News Nightline." Greene has written nine previous books, including the national bestsellers BE TRUE TO YOUR SCHOOL and GOOD MORNING, MERRY SUNSHINE.